Let's Talk Wine!

Marc Chapleau

Let's Talk
Wine!

An expert takes on your questions

XYZ
Publishing

National Library of Canada Cataloguing in Publication

Chapleau, Marc

    Let's talk wine! : an expert takes on your questions

    Translation of: À nous deux le vin!

Includes an index

    ISBN 1-894852-07-9

    1. Wine and wine making. 2. Wine tasting. I. Title.

TP548.C52313 2003   641.2'2   C2003-941687-9

Legal Deposit: Fourth quarter 2003
National Library of Canada
Bibliothèque nationale du Québec

XYZ Publishing acknowledges the financial support our publishing program receives from the Book Publishing Industry Development Program (BPIDP) of the Department of Canadian Heritage and the Société de développement des entreprises culturelles.

Translator: Darcy Dunton
Editor: Rhonda Bailey
Layout: Édiscript enr.
Layout design: Christine Charette
Cover design: Zirval Design
Cover photo: Sylvie Guernon

Printed and bound in Canada

XYZ Publishing
1781 Saint Hubert Street
Montreal, Quebec H2L 3Z1
Tel: (514) 525-2170
Fax: (514) 525-7537
E-mail: info@xyzedit.qc.ca
Web site: www.xyzedit.qc.ca

Distributed by: Fitzhenry & Whiteside
195 Allstate Parkway
Markham, ON L3R 4T8
Customer Service, tel: (905) 477-9700
Toll free ordering, tel: 1-800-387-9776
Fax: 1-800-260-9777
E-mail: bookinfo@fitzhenry.ca

[Contents]

[List of Tables]

[Foreword]

Taking On Wine

I n other words, it's time to roll up your sleeves and grapple with this worthy challenger. At the end of the bout, satisfied and replete, you'll be able to drink to your good fortune and to the quadrupled pleasure you'll find in drinking wine when it's been demystified once and for all.

I can't count the number of people who have approached me over the years – and they still do, every day – to ask me all sorts of questions about wine. Although their queries range from basic to very sophisticated, all of these people seem to be intimidated by the subject and by the eternal mystique that, in their eyes, is connected to this noble beverage.

Thus, it was both to reassure my fellow wine drinkers and to throw some light on certain areas of darkness for them that I decided to write this book. With a menu composed of 120 questions and answers, even confirmed wine lovers will discover things they had never imagined.

The fictional scenarios leading into the different topics are meant to illustrate some of the ways in which wine and wine culture not only liven up everyday existence, but also pursue their adepts into the most unexpected corners of their lives.

[Section 1]
Tasting Wine

⌈The Diagnosis

"Sorry to use an old cliché, my friend, but your condition really does lend itself to it: I've got some good news and some bad news for you."

"Give me the good news, doctor, quick!"

"Nothing worrying has turned up in the tests or in your check-up – absolutely no sign of serious disease. You're in excellent shape, I'm afraid. However…"

"Now I'm in for it!"

"Tsk, tsk. You have anosmia, that's all. Acquired anosmia, it appears."

"Is *that* why I haven't been able to…?"

"Why you can hardly taste anything, and can't smell anything at all – neither the great Burgundy you told me about last Christmas, nor the rosé I see sticking out of your gym bag. You've lost your sense of smell! Not 100%, only about 80% of it. Don't despair: with a little adaptation, you'll live to be a hundred! Even if the problem doesn't suddenly go away, which often happens…"

■ Is everyone capable of fully tasting wine?

U nless they're afflicted by anosmia, yes, practically everyone can learn to taste wine properly and even become reasonably good at it. Of course, some people are more gifted than others; perhaps their senses are sharper. But, as celebrated wine expert Émile Peynaud[1] once pointed out,

---

1. Nonagenarian Émile Peynaud is considered one of the fathers of modern oenology. During his lengthy career, he has acted as adviser to the top Bordeaux wineries.

"Rarely does this advantage extend to all flavours and all odours."

Peynaud affirms that the average person can become a wine connoisseur. This is certainly encouraging, and reaffirms the democratic character of wine – its accessibility and its congeniality.

What, then, accounts for the fact that some individuals are better at singling out aromas right from the start, and learn the subtleties of wine tasting very quickly? The key lies in their enthusiasm: their interest in wine and their pleasure in drinking it. Another essential, common-sense factor is practice.

Good recall power must also be mentioned: the ability to store our impressions of a wine in our memories – if not the exact taste of a particular bottle, at least its general character as a representative of a certain type. Memory, or recognition, is the greatest ally of wine tasters. It allows us to make comparisons and, among other things, to identify the grape varieties that have been used to make the wine in our glass.

Thus, the equation is roughly the following: a normal sense of smell and taste + interest in the subject matter + a sharp and accurate memory + perseverance + an inquiring mind + assiduous practice + the desire to share = a discriminating wine buff in the making.

This may seem demanding, but in most cases, almost all the prerequisites are already present in a dormant state; you just need to awaken them. The difficulty is that many people refuse to accept the idea that an activity as simple as raising a glass to their lips and drinking from it requires having to learn to taste again from scratch, as if they were babies learning to use a cup.

Yes, relearning is necessary; we won't pretend otherwise.

Go ahead and taste proactively, to use a popular term from the business world. Without making a big production out of it, you can focus on keeping your senses on the alert. Sample two kinds of old cheddar, one with a smoother texture; two cups of tea, one of which has been steeped a few minutes longer than the other; semi-sweet chocolate and chocolate that is 80% pure cacao. Let yourself go, and have fun making these comparisons.

On Your Knees

This oration to Bacchus has proved infallible. Recite twice over, on four consecutive days:

"Oh deity of the vine, splendour of the heavens, king of grape varieties and father of all oenophiles, aid me in my quest! Son of Zeus, brother-in-law of Dionysus, god of wine and merrymaking, grant my plea to become a wine connoisseur. Take me with you, oh Bacchus, but deliver me from carousing, bacchanalia, and debauchery!"

When your goal is achieved, don't forget to be suitably grateful and publish your acknowledgement of the deity's intervention in the classified section of the newspaper.

I'm really interested in wine. Sometimes I think I can identify an aroma or two. I want to become more knowledgeable about it, but how should I begin a real initiation? What is a good starting point?

First of all, you should examine your motives. Do you want to plunge headlong into the domain simply because it's a status symbol to be known as an appreciator of good wine? Is it just a whim, a personal fantasy, or a sudden passion? If so, you'll probably still succeed in making strides quite rapidly. However, as is often observed, your interest may wane just as quickly as it arose.

Let's presume that you are sincerely interested and authentically curious about wine.

The first concrete step in a proactive approach to tasting is to pay close attention to the taste of everything that ends up on your table: coffee, a sauce or a dip, even crackers! Are they too sour, or too salty?

Are they crisp enough, does pepper dominate the other flavours, and is there really a hint of cinnamon in them? Without boring your dinner partners to tears, take a moment to express your opinion, even a general one, about what you are eating and drinking. Don't hesitate to compare your impressions with companions sharing the same fare.

At the same time, take notes, even a few hastily scrawled words, so that you'll retain the name of the wine drunk on a particular occasion – not later than the day after, however, or you'll probably be forced to sheepishly admit that you've forgotten its name, even though you can swear that the label was blue and green. Unless you have a phenomenal memory, note-taking is essential. It also helps you to be able to concentrate and describe the wine's colour, aromas, and flavours as succinctly and accurately as possible, even if you scribble your own personal shorthand. Buy a notebook and keep it handy so that you can grab it whenever you open and taste a new bottle of wine. Instead of viewing this as a chore, pamper yourself by spending a few moments alone with the wine in the kitchen, as long as the cooking odours are not too invasive.

Better still (although this may not always go smoothly), share your wine experiments with a tasting partner – your husband, wife, lover, friend, or – why not? – one of your children who is old enough to drink. Even if the other person is not as committed to learning about wine as you are, he or she can corroborate your impressions, challenge them, or enjoy practising one-upmanship, especially when your selection turns out to be a pain in the liver.

If you're necessarily alone in your tasting adventure, a beginners' wine course is a wonderful solution. Well-prepared courses, given in a friendly, relaxed atmosphere, are available in most cities throughout the year; your neighbourhood liquor board or wine store will probably have information about them. Also, wine writers recommend reputable wine courses every so often in their newspaper and magazine columns.

The last crucial pointer for you at the beginning of your quest is to read the label thoroughly. A veritable wine ID-card, the label contains a mine of information that will give you a good idea of where you're headed with the wine you're about to drink.

Haunting the aisles of the larger liquor commissions or wine stores, discussing wine with staff advisers, and peeking at the choices made by other customers who look as enthusiastic as you do: these are all ways to familiarize yourself with wine, wine lovers, and their universe, bringing you a new awareness and sensitivity.

The world you are about to enter is not only a world of aromas and flavours, but also a repository of fascinating aspects of geology, geography, history, chemistry, sociology, and even philosophy and ethics (e.g., the controversy over genetically-modified vines).

Definitions to Ponder When Tasting Wine
(from the Oxford English Dictionary)

Expectation: mentally waiting for something; anticipating something to be received; a preconceived idea or opinion with regard to what will take place; supposition.

Attentiveness: steadily applying one's mind, observant faculties or energies; giving or evincing careful consideration; heedful, observant.

The label has been scrutinized, and calm reigns at the table. The glass, one-third full, is ready for auscultation. What happens now?

Without a conscious effort on your part, nothing will happen. No revelation will hit you like a bolt from the blue. The glass contains only wine – nothing more exotic than fermented grape juice, after all – and you are about to taste it. The ball is in your court; wine tasting is not a passive activity.

Once that is established, your proactive tasting should be done in three stages: first, assess the wine's appearance – its colour and limpidity, second, its aromas, and finally, its flavours. In other words, the eye, the nose, and the mouth. It's as simple as that.

THE EYE: These days – thank goodness – it is extremely rare that the consumer is confronted with a bottle, even one costing under $10, that contains turbid wine. Nonetheless, it's still worthwhile to take the wine's colour into consideration.

Is it limpid and clear? Or, on the contrary, is it rather murky? Is the colour attractive, bright and luminous? To appreciate this important aspect of wine, hold the glass against a white (neutral) background – a napkin or a piece of paper – to note its relative richness of tone and to see whether it is semi-opaque (as some young ports should be) or noticeably pale (as expected in rosés and Beaujolais Nouveau). A red wine that is so dark it is impossible to see through it is not necessarily better than a pale-coloured one, which, although it is sure to be lighter in body, may be more refined, more nuanced, and more pleasant to drink in the long run.

THE NOSE: We're getting closer to the heart of the matter. First, smell the wine without swirling it in the glass (as you have surely seen other people doing). Certain aromas should already be perceptible – although it occasionally happens that a wine with little or no aroma is in a mute, or closed phase. Then, air the wine by swirling it. The oxygen captured by the moving wine encourages aromas to rise from it.

To swirl, place the glass flat on the table. Rotate it rapidly in a complete circle, counter-clockwise (clockwise if you're left-handed). The best way to do this is to rest your forearm on the table, holding your elbow close to your side for better control (this is important). Don't be discouraged if you make a mess at first. With a little practice, in no time you'll be able to confidently swirl your wine glass in the air when necessary, even in the middle of a banquet.

Tip No. 1: The nose tires quickly. It's pointless to keep smelling the wine in your glass over and over, hoping to capture elusive aromas. On the other hand, an effective technique to instantly regenerate your sense of smell is to discreetly sniff your hand or your sleeve (if you're dressed).

Tip No. 2: Don't expect to find all the smells you detect engaging and agreeable right off the bat. Some aged red Burgundies, for example, smell of decay. But accept the possibility that you'll eventually get to like this somewhat musty odour. Just as you may have loathed turnips and spinach when you were a child, as a novice wine lover you may not appreciate some of the stronger sensations at first. You have to get used to them; you *will* get used to them, as long as you keep a positive attitude.

Tip No. 3: As we will see later, at a low estimate, there are several hundred aromatic components teeming in your glass of wine. So, if you think you smell marijuana smoke, don't look around to find the culprit: some wine does release an aroma reminiscent of cannabis. Some tasters would call this scent dried grass or new-mown hay.

Wine writers unanimously and emphatically stress that you should go with your first impression when tasting. If the idea of roses flashes into your mind when your nose is plunged inside your glass, it is almost certainly because the wine in question *does* smell like roses, among other things.

Unfortunately, many people balk at trusting this inner voice. They prefer to be reassured, and above all, are mortally afraid of looking ridiculous by naming an aroma that no one else in the room has detected. The only cure for this lack of confidence is practice and more practice, which will soon put an end to faltering hesitations.

I should mention here that the majority of the good wine tasters I have known over the last twenty years stand out precisely because of their lack of hesitation. In fact, they are quite brazen. They're not afraid of failure, nor of being the butt of gibes. They even laugh it off when they're exposed as being completely off base, identifying a

Bordeaux as a Burgundy in a blind tasting session, for instance. And their fellow tasters usually laugh heartily along with them.

In short, we don't always learn from our errors, but we're none the worse for it.

THE MOUTH: This is where it's at – with all due respect to those who hold that the nose and the wine's bouquet are sufficient unto themselves.

It would take several pages to analyze the gustative process in all its innumerable facets and its multiple snares. The main thing to be aware of is that if you hold your nose while chewing and swallowing a morsel of food, it doesn't have any taste at all. We taste food thanks to the odiferous vapours that it gives off and which make their way to the nose through the back of the mouth. Holding the nose cuts off the updraft, like blocking a chimney, and prevents the odours from reaching the olfactory bulb. Instead, they go right down the gullet, undetected.

Although there is still some controversy on the subject in scientific circles, it is believed that the tongue and taste buds cannot distinguish much more than the four principal taste sensations: sweetness (the front of the tongue, near the tip), acidity (posterior sides), bitterness (the back), and saltiness (sides, at the front).[2]

Thus, once the wine is in the mouth, besides the aromas that reach our consciousness via the olfactory bulb, we are assessing the wine's texture and body, and the relative strength of each of the four basic sensations detected by our taste buds, as well as the balance between these elements.

The technique of noisily sucking in air while tasting wine is the equivalent of fanning the fire in a fireplace, sending in air to help the

2. It has been said that no salt taste exists in wine and that there is no point in exploring this sensory area with respect to wine. However, tasters frequently detect a prickle of salt, even in some red wines. The salt taste is not disagreeable if it blends well with the aromas and flavours of the wine; it is most likely due to the presence of mineral salts, reflecting the influence of the terroir (particular climate and soil where the grapes are grown).

aromas rise up the "chimney" so they can be detected by our sense of smell. Wine tasters do this quite often, but it is not indispensable at the beginning – let's say the first six months – of your apprenticeship as a serious wine lover.

The famous length, or finish, of a wine is often an enigma for beginners, defying their understanding. This quality, also known as aromatic persistence, is generally restricted to fine wines and almost never applies to ordinary ones, except in a negative sense, when a wine seems diluted (like coffee when too much water has dripped through the filter). In this case, when the taste abruptly vanishes as soon as it is swallowed, the wine is referred to as "short."

[Dos and Don'ts To Enhance Your Wine-Tasting Skills]

Do:

- Find a tasting partner. If no flesh-and-blood one is willing and able, you might find a virtual tasting buddy on the Internet.
- Carry out your tasting exercises regularly.
- Talk about wine in a sober, serious manner, but also fearlessly and confidently.
- Taste at opportune moments, when you are calm, rested, and well-disposed.
- Use the appropriate kind of wine glass.
- Take the necessary time to concentrate and give your full attention to tasting.
- Taste certain wines over and over again to note your progress in discernment.

Don't:

- Wear perfume or cologne while tasting wine, or sit beside someone who "smells nice."
- Attribute too much importance to the colour of the wine.
- Rely entirely on your memory instead of taking notes.
- Censure your impressions because of excessive modesty or good manners.
- Pose as a voluble and pretentious wine expert, cheating by speaking insincerely.
- Fill the glass more than a third full.
- Drink red wine at room temperature (19-22°C, or 66-71°F).
- Loudly broadcast your impressions, before the people with you have had time to reach their own conclusions.

Detective Skills

I hadn't been on a job for four months. My bills were piling up to the ceiling, the new police chief was squeezing me for some evidence, and it was hotter than hell in my office. My feet were up on my desk and I was nursing a cold beer, vacantly contemplating the letters that read (backwards) "Dick Tremblay, Private Detective" through the textured glass of my office door. At that moment, the door swung open and a statuesque blond of the kind you only see in your dreams strode into the room and sat down opposite me.

Without saying a word, she opened a little valise and brought out a cut-glass container full of an unidentified red liquid. While I struggled to get my feet down without losing my dignity, she cleared a space amid the mess on my desk and placed the decanter on it.

"Let's see if you're as good as they say you are," she said. And, producing a glass from her case, she poured some of the red liquid into it until it was a quarter full – a teetotaller's portion! She handed it to me with a sweep of her arm and looked me in the eye.

"I'm leaving you the decanter, the glass, and my card. When you've figured out what kind of wine this is, call me. Don't rush it: rinse the beer out of your mouth first! If you succeed in solving this 'case,' I think we'll be able to do things together. Goodbye... Dick."

She smiled at me before she walked out and left me staring at the closed door, dazed. I squinted at the elegant, gold-rimmed card: "Countess Véronique Duplantez de Barry, Ph.D., Chief Oenologist, Vinifera Estate."

■ What is a blind tasting?

The glass in front of you contains red wine. There is no trace of the bottle, label, cork, capsule, or any other clue that could help you identify it. The grinning individual across the table invites you to "taste this one" and to give your opinion on what it might be. You are being asked to do a blind tasting.

You have to trust entirely to your memory and to your powers of deduction to try to guess the wine's regional origin, or – much more difficult – its specific identity: the name of the vintner, the appellation or the growth, and the vintage[3].

The colour will give you a preliminary indication of the wine's age. The purplish tinge of young red wine gradually gives way to orange, and finally brown tones over time. The nose will also provide a clue about relative age: red wines smell of fruit when they are young and acquire earthy scents of mushrooms and undergrowth as they age. In the mouth, still referring to red wine, flavours tend to lose flesh, becoming smoother and more supple when the wine has aged sufficiently, but hasn't yet dried out.

This kind of recognizable progression, and the earmarks used in blind tasting in general, are mainly valid for great wines that have a strong character and are therefore more easily identified. But even then, there are always pitfalls in blind tasting. As I mentioned before, even experienced tasters get very different types of wine mixed up every so often. This kind of faux pas may seem colossal, but it's par for the course for tasters, and shows how wine can teach us humility.

---

3. "Growth" (*cru*, in French) is a category used in France to designate certain good-quality vineyards, and by extension, the wines produced from them. The word is also used simply as a synonym of fine wine. Classified growths possess official status and are ranked in hierarchical order, starting with *grand cru* (great growth) or *premier cru* (first growth), according to the wine region, since these ranking terms differ slightly among regions, down to fifth growth (in the particular case of Bordeaux). The terms *grand cru* and *premier cru* refer to excellent vineyard sites, and therefore, in principal (see page 154-155), to excellent wines. The different appellations, on the other hand, apply almost everywhere in Europe, and guarantee that a wine has been produced in a particular place, according to determined (legislated) rules (see page 153).

If blind tasting is essentially a guessing game – just a show, where luck can tip the scale – then what about those sommeliers who manage to get the exact names of wines in tasting contests? Is there a middle ground between the two extremes?

Blind tasting is far from an exercise in futility. On the contrary: it's wonderful training for recognizing and effectively memorizing the typical aromas and flavours of specific wines. Deprived of the support of a label, which often tells us in advance what we ought to smell or taste, we must rely strictly on our senses. Free of the value judgments that result from even a cursory glance at the label, we won't be swayed by the prestige or lack of prestige associated with a particular name.

TIP: If you want to amuse yourself carrying out blind tastings, the trick is to not try to guess the mystery wine's identity straight away. Instead, you should proceed by elimination: "It's certainly not a Beaujolais (too dark) or a Bordeaux (too juicy)," and so forth, until you narrow it down to a likely possibility.

Some of us tasters like to determine from the outset whether we are tasting a New World or an Old World wine. The former are generally darker in colour and fleshier than the latter, and have a sweeter taste of ripe fruit. Once that is established, the search can focus on the country of origin ("It's too astringent for a French wine; it must be Italian"), then the region ("It's too alcoholic and concentrated to be from a temperate region").

An intelligent blind tasting session should provide general information about the type of wine being presented ("Taste this one: it's a Bordeaux. But I won't give anything else away."). This saves people from making the most humiliating kind of mistakes, and is a good compromise between the total blind tasting, in which nothing at all is known about the wine, and one in which too much is revealed for it to be an instructive challenge.

One last point: some wine writers have said that the term "anonymous" should be used instead of "blind," as the taster is not blindfolded, after all, but simply in the dark about the mystery wine's name (and therefore, its origin and type). However the word "blind" has long been a consecrated expression in the wine-tasting milieu, and is accurate in that tasters must rely almost totally on senses other than sight, namely, smell and taste.

At the Marriage Counsellor's

"I'm at my wits' end! My wife and I have always been so close – we've never had any serious problems until now. She's become obsessed with wine lately, and things have started to go downhill between us. According to her, it's never the right time; any excuse is valid to stop me from expressing my passion. I'm a genius in the kitchen, you see, but lately, in the middle of preparing a new gourmet recipe, I've had to stop everything on the stove because she's trying out a new Madiran! She can't stand vulgar cooking odours interfering with her noble quest..."

■ What are the ideal conditions for tasting wine?

It makes sense that to properly appreciate wine, first of all, you should be in good physical health – especially not suffering from a cold, which completely knocks out your sense of smell. Also, a good state of bodily health usually implies a good state of mind, making it more likely that you will be open and receptive. If not, you will probably miss out on enjoying some great wines, simply because you won't notice many of their qualities.

A second important point is that our tasting abilities – with respect to wine as much as any other food or drink – are at their sharpest just before lunch or dinner, when we are working up an appetite and our senses are on the alert. Wine experts usually do their tasting between ten in the morning and one o'clock in the afternoon, or in the early evening, between five and seven. At home, in your everyday routine, it's easier to assess wine before the meal is served, or even before cooking it, or heating it up.

A modicum of peace and quiet is obviously desirable, or at least an absence of disturbance. Professional tastings often unfold in a monastic silence so that participants will not be influenced by their colleagues' reactions, even non-verbal ones.

Thus, in general terms, the important thing is that the tasting occur in surroundings that allow your full concentration, with the least possible amount of distraction.

[Halloween Night

"Good Lord! Did you see Henry's outfit?"

"The invitation said 'costumes,' so what's the problem?"

"Come on, have you ever seen such a get-up? Fruit on his head, that netting passing for a mail tunic, gravel and sand stuck all over his legs, earth falling out of his hair! And those ridiculous 3-D glasses he's giving people to look at him!"

"You're just jealous. You must admit, it was a brilliant idea to come as a *grand cru*!"

■ How do we recognize a great wine?

A straight question deserves a straight answer. It's impossible, or practically impossible, to recognize a great wine without a considerable amount of tasting experience and a close acquaintance with a wide range of appellations and the diverse types of wine that are produced in the major wine-growing regions of the world.

Even then, great wines take you by surprise. Both amateurs and professionals (who have sampled an extraordinary variety of wines) are thrown for a loop when they encounter that awesome treat for the eye, nose, and palate. Not only does it taste very good, but it carries off the astonishing tour de force of strongly impressing the senses without falling into caricature, that is, without being particularly full-bodied or having a very pronounced flavour.

Another characteristic of a great wine is its entrancing complexity. It releases a multitude of aromas, and its flavour is a revelation at every mouthful, regardless of the food you may be eating or your level of receptivity. In sum, great wine is complex, multiform, and multi-dimensional.

An expensive wine is not necessarily a great wine. On the other hand, a great wine is never cheap!

An attentive, open-minded wine lover will immediately know, without any advance warning, that he or she is in the presence of a precious and rare gem.

[The Ruined Dinner Party

Turi and Sasha's anniversary party started off well. The guests were a good mix, and the music in the background created a relaxed atmosphere.

The *plat de résistance* was beyond criticism: succulent but not flamboyant, it was ideal for the star wine of the evening.

But, horror of horrors! Contrary to all expectations, the Château Montrose was a terrible letdown, with no bouquet to speak of, and mute as far as flavour was concerned. The prestigious Bordeaux simply refused to unveil itself. Needless to say, this shocking development, equally embarrassing for hosts and guests, cast a pall over the festivities...

▌ How can we tell if a wine is too young and ▌ needs more time in the bottle?

The key indicator is depth. A promising but too-young wine may be mute, or closed, but you can sense (and taste) that it is capable of achieving much more if it is relatively tight-knit and concentrated in flavour and aroma. A white wine will eventually open up and show its stuff as long as it has enough acidity. If it is red, it must possess enough good tannins, without necessarily being harsh. Some astringency is desirable, since the presence of acidity ensures a greater longevity to the whole. And in both cases, balance – or better still, harmony – among the components constitutes an excellent prognostic.

We can deduce by tasting that a wine will go a long way, but it's also a matter of feeling, of intuition and inner conviction. Wine is alive; it is constantly evolving and can go in one direction or the other at any moment, either dashing our most fervent hopes or miraculously resuscitating, even when the funeral arrangements have already been made.

Except in a blind tasting when we don't know the wine's pedigree, the reputation of the estate, vineyard, château, or vintage is an additional indicator of whether or not a wine has the potential to improve by spending a few more years in the cellar.

Tip: When you don't feel like waiting for a wine to reach its peak, decanting it may give it more suppleness, stir up its aromas and tame the youthful ardour of its tannins.

[House Debate

"Mr. Speaker, in concluding, I call upon Parliament and all the members of this august assembly to vote with their hearts, their souls, and their consciences. It is rare, exceedingly rare, that we have the opportunity to vote freely, unfettered by party discipline. The matter that we must decide on today is the following: 'In the name of Canadian unity and in accord with the Canadian Charter of Rights and Freedoms, do we officially recognize sexual equality in the matter of wine-tasting aptitude?'"

Do women make better wine tasters than men?

The answer to this contentious question is yes, in that women are often more spontaneous and intuitive than men. Women also recognize certain smells more easily than men do. They are more intimately familiar with the fruit, spice, and floral scents that go into making perfumes and cosmetics. Moreover, before men discovered the joy of cooking, women ruled the kitchen and were closer to the thousand and one odours that filled not only the kitchen and pantry, but the entire house. Only during the last few decades have they relinquished their exclusive rule over this domain.

In practice, male and female wine tasters show equal skill, although researchers have found that women's sense of smell is more acute, possibly for hormonal reasons.

The only advantage that men may have over women in this area is that they have a greater propensity to rationalize and organize their sensations, and above all, to infer a multitude of considerations from them, of the type: "I'll try it again in six months;" "the wine maker was pretty heavy-handed with the oak;" "I wonder what rating it got from Parker;"[4] "I must remember to have four bottles put aside as soon as possible;" etc.

⸢In Memoriam

"Suddenly, in Nelson, B.C., on September 20, 2003, at the age of 57, Mr. Léoville Barton. He leaves to mourn his faithful companion, Marik L'Allier des Vosges, as well as many descendants and innumerable admirers. There will be no visitation. The wishes of the deceased to be recycled will be respected. No flowers, and absolutely no perfume, please. Donations to the World Foundation for Cork Sickness will be appreciated. Wine connoisseurs and other lovers of the good things in life are asked to take note of his passing and to lobby, as aggressively as possible, for the eradication of this terrible plague which is carrying off the most meritorious elements of our society."

■ How does one recognize corked wine?

By its characteristic odour, followed by confirmation in the mouth. Corked wine smells musty and dank. This is not necessarily a repulsive odour in itself. Moreover, the wine may be affected to a greater or lesser degree, making the detection of cork taint quite difficult, even for the experts.

---

4. American wine writer Robert Parker's opinions on wine have reigned supreme for more than fifteen years. Wine growers will go to any length, including selling their souls to the Devil, to produce the fleshy, concentrated wines that will receive a tip of his hat and consequently sell like hotcakes.

In practice, the phenomenon comes to our attention in the following way. When smelling the wine, we are struck by the absence of fruity, spicy, floral, or woody scents. Instead, the wine has an "off" smell, commonly described as an odour of wet cardboard, wet newspaper, or damp basement.

"It isn't clean," is the appropriate expression of shocked disappointment when this occurs. Sometimes, when the corkiness is not pronounced enough for the wine to be declared adulterated, you should taste it again more attentively: the wine's strangeness may be due to another factor, possibly poorly maintained barrels which have given it a mouldy taste.

On the palate, corked wine manifests itself by a thin, dried-out flavour. It will also be "short," that is, its taste will vanish as soon as it is swallowed. Once it suffers from cork sickness, a wine is irretrievably spoiled.[5] Even if you air the wine by decanting, the musty smell cannot be eliminated – on the contrary, it will intensify. Nevertheless, some people will find that the wine is still drinkable, and a few even swear by this dank odour, imagining that it is an integral component of the wine that gives it a desirable whiff of old cellar!

Whatever these people's tastes may be, the fact remains that corked wine does not offer us the sought-after fruit that makes up the essence of good wine – the delightful aromas of apricot, peach, black currant, cherry, strawberry, or raspberry.

■ Where does the corked taste come from?

Cork sickness is a complex phenomenon, and the debate about it is not over yet. It is difficult to finger the specific cause in every case. It may be transmitted via contaminated

---

5. If, for some reason, you can't take the bottle back to the wine store or liquor commission for a refund, corked wine is said to be safe for use in the kitchen.

corks, but probably more often than we think, it comes from the wood of the barrels, casks, or vats, or even from the wood used to build the wine storage facilities. It is believed that the chemical compound (2,4,6-trichloroanisole, or TCA) responsible for this problem can remain suspended in the air in the winery, ready to attach itself to the cork and attack the wine.

The main problem is that it is impossible to tell with the naked eye whether or not a natural cork has been affected. The cork may appear flawless, without cracks, fissures, or holes, yet it may harbour the taint, and harmful interaction between its components and those of the wine will ensue.

Where the canker gnaws for wine lovers in general and for the wine industry in particular is that it takes only an infinitesimal amount of TCA to contaminate wine and cause it to take on a corked taste. And this detestable, overwhelming odour is all the more unwelcome these days, when wine makers are striving to produce fruity, mellow wines as opposed to harsh, drying ones.

Although the statistics vary a lot according to place, we can estimate the proportion of bottles of corked wine on the shelves of wine stores today at approximately 7%. This is enormous in terms of the sheer number of bottles, and represents one out of every fourteen bottles. Any other industry that bore such a high proportion of defective products in its total output would have collapsed a long time ago!

This is a good illustration of wine's strong power of attraction – its capacity to maintain and even increase its appeal in spite of adversity.

■ Isn't there a cure for corked wine?

Traditionalists might find the idea offensive, but the metal screw-on cap appears to provide the best protection against the phenomenon of cork-tainted wine – until now, at any rate. By means of an inner joint of inert material, it makes the bottle perfectly airtight; no element causing any off-taste or spoilage can contaminate it.

Opponents to the use of the metal cap for wine object that it destroys a poetic aspect of wine-drinking: the sacred (or secular) ritual of uncorking the bottle. To them, it would be unthinkable for a *grand cru* to be opened by unscrewing a cap as if it were a vulgar bottle of soda pop.

A more concrete disadvantage of capping is that the wine in the bottle cannot "breathe" as it does through natural cork. Research has shown that a microscopic quantity of air seeps through a cork – not really enough to influence the aging process, although the last word on this subject has not yet been said, nor is it likely to be said any time soon. The researchers are presumably still hard at work on it.

Artificial corks of synthetic resin or polyethylene are really quite effective substitutes for the real thing. We see them more and more frequently in the necks of wine bottles from all over the world, and this option may be a good course to follow in the future. On the other hand, it has been found that they transmit a taste of vinyl to the wine after about a year in the bottle. Also, unfortunately, an Australian study has shown that even synthetically corked wines can be contaminated and spoiled by the insidious TCA molecule.

[Old Tasting Partners

"This is pathetic. Give up!"

"Hold on... it'll come in a minute, you'll see!"

The speaker plunged his nose into his wine glass again and again, sniffing rapidly every time. He took another gulp of wine and sloshed it around in his mouth, noisily.

"Well?" demanded his crony, "Isn't it a bit salty? – if you ever get a bead on it!"

"I don't know! And what wouldn't I *give* to know! But, wait… yes, it is salty, almost unbearably salty for that matter!"

"Let's face it, old pal, our taste buds are losing it!"

Does our wine-tasting ability diminish as we grow older?

Our smell and taste acuity are at their best when we are between the ages of thirty and sixty. Over sixty, both of these faculties gradually lose their sharpness. This is why many older people sprinkle a lot of salt on their food: they can barely detect saltiness – a taste that is present in some wines.

Another widely accepted scientific finding is that cigarette smokers have a less discriminating sense of smell (and therefore, taste) than non-smokers. The fact is, however, you'll run into a number well-aged wine tasters who have never given up their smoking habit, yet remain quite adept at tasting. Perhaps their senses have adapted or compensated, like a person who has lost the use of the right arm and learns to perform marvels with the left; we don't know for certain.

As it is, a reputable French scientific journal stated recently, in all seriousness: "It's better that a smoker not refrain from indulging the vice before tasting wine, or he or she may be less receptive."[6]

---

6. *Sciences et Avenir*, No. 120, Oct./Nov., 1999

⌈Spitting Out the Good With the Bad

"Look! Quick, over there! – you missed it again."

"What *are* you talking about?"

"That man standing near the table: he doesn't seem to like any of the wine samples."

"Why do you say that?"

"Every time he takes a sip, he spits it into that brown garbage pail."

"Gross!"

▌How can we taste wine properly if we spit it out?

S pitting out the wine does not detract from tasting it. In any case, after the tongue and taste buds have come into contact with the wine and the aromas have risen to the nose via the retronasal passage, nothing much happens from a sensory point of view when the wine (beer, coffee, or even cod liver oil!) goes down the throat.

Naturally, an important part of drinking wine with dinner, or having a beer while leaning on a bar counter, is the act of swallowing, simply for the satisfaction of it. At a wine-tasting session, on the other hand, professionals who must evaluate seven or eight different wines in a row are obliged to spit out every mouthful they sample, imbibing as little alcohol as possible so they won't be guilty of impaired tasting. After all, they aren't drinking for pleasure, but to give their expert opinions on a technical subject!

If there were a way to subjugate the effects of alcohol, you can be sure that even the most effete wine taster wouldn't hesitate to drink down all, or almost all of the samples tasted. The cruellest aspect of a wine taster's job is having to spit out a mouthful of an excellent *grand cru*!

The actual spitting is no easy matter either although some novices succeed in expelling a lovely, powerful arc on their first try, by no merit of their own, inciting envy among their less fortunate friends.. To avoid making a mess, purse your lips, try rolling the end of your tongue into a U-shape (if you can: this is an inherited talent), take aim and project the liquid. Practise at home first, in front of the kitchen sink, and don't give up: it took me fifteen years to get it right!

[Section 2]
Talking About Wine

[e-mail

Subject: Help!
From: <anonymous@winebuff.ca.>
To: <guru@onwine.com>

"Dear Wine Guru,
I'm writing you as a last resort, hoping you can solve my problem. I lead an active social life. I like to dress well and make a good impression. I enjoy good food and drink, as well as good company. I don't claim to be an expert, but I appreciate fine wines. The problem is, I can never think of anything intelligent to say about them! When someone asks me my opinion of the wine we're drinking at a restaurant or a dinner party, I'm suddenly at a total loss. My face turns bright red and all I can come out with is: 'Yes, it... it's good... very good.' I try to save face by grabbing the bottle and scanning the label. Then I'll say something stupid like: 'Oh... I see, it's a... voss-nay romanee.' Can you help me, or should I give up wine altogether?"

Is there an easy formula for describing wine – a few catchwords that I can use to sum up a wine's qualities without having to memorize a tasting glossary?

Yes, there is a way. For instance, you can describe a red wine adequately simply by choosing either "light," "robust," or "very robust," depending on the intensity of the flavour.

People who are just beginning to explore the world of wine tend not to appreciate full-bodied reds, which are often very rich from the point of view of colour (dark), aroma (powerful), and flavour (strong). This is reflected in the selection of wines sold in convenience stores and supermarkets: they are rarely more than medium-bodied; in fact, most are light-bodied. This is deliberate, given that most people who decide to buy their wine at a convenience store are not wine connoisseurs in the making. Usually, they just want a mildly intoxicating liquid that goes down easily with food.

In the case of white wines, where the variety is narrower than for reds, you'll be safe, if you're a beginner, if you limit your comments to either "light-" or "full-bodied," with a footnote on the relative sweetness or dryness of the wine. The observations regarding the colour of red wines are valid for whites as well: the deeper the colour (going towards dark yellow, golden, or topaz), the more likely it is that the wine will be full-bodied, rich, and high in alcohol content.

Can you provide a slightly fuller range of basic terms that encompass the wine-tasting experience?

Here are the essential ones, with brief explanations.
BODY: The "weight," volume and density of the wine in the mouth, mainly a tactile sensation. A comparison with a cup of strong coffee helps to convey what the feel of a full-bodied wine is like, in contrast to a light-bodied wine, which would correspond to a cup of weak coffee ("dishwater," if you like).[1]

---

1. Analogy is used in many domains besides wine. Music is sometimes described as "rich," "rounded," or "enveloping," terms which convey an atmosphere, along with the word "warm." Aroma analogies work by subjective impressions rather than by rationalistic definitions, but this does not make them less valid for evocative purposes.

CORKED: The taste of wine adulterated by contamination, usually transmitted by a tainted cork; tastes almost exclusively of wet cardboard; dank, mouldy.

FRUIT and FRUITY: Except for Muscat, wine rarely smells like grape juice, but it releases fruity aromas and has flavours ranging from cherry, raspberry, plum, peach, apricot, apple, and black currant to pineapple and passion fruit. Note that "fruity," when describing wine, doesn't mean sweet.

LENGTH: When a wine's taste lingers in the mouth after swallowing, it is said to possess length. Bulk wines almost never achieve length, or (its synonyms) persistence, a long finish, aftertaste, etc. A wine is "short" if its taste disappears as soon as it is swallowed. The novice wine buff shouldn't be alarmed if he or she cannot distinguish length in the mouth within the first few weeks of conscientious tasting.

MOUTH (or PALATE): The taste of wine in the mouth. You might say, for instance: "Disappointing in the mouth, thin and dried out; probably corked," or, "the nose is unimpressive, but it redeems itself on the palate with good, jammy black currant and a long finish."

NOSE: Simply put, the smell of wine. A supernose? The wine not only smells good, but literally explodes with aromas. This is a reason for rejoicing, especially if the price is reasonable. And the opposite case – a closed nose, a wine that has no perceptible smell at all? This does occur, whereas if another year or two had passed before the bottle was opened, it might have been a different story.

OXIDIZED: Once the wine is bottled, it cannot tolerate air and oxygen. This is why airtight stoppers (corks and other kinds of seals) are used to close it. Once the bottle has been opened, the wine will begin to oxidize, and eventually, the aromas will dissipate, the colour will darken and dull, and the wine will be irretrievably spoiled.

TANNIN: This substance, of vegetable origin, exists almost exclusively in red wines. If the tannins are not ripe enough, or if there is an excess of tannin, the wine will have a rough or harsh quality. Strong tea that has been steeped too long, causing a mouth-puckering dryness, is referred to as tannic. Tannins are essential to red wine, giving it structure and balance. Tannins are to reds what acidity is to whites: the backbone of the wine. To have a good idea of a tannic wine, try a bottle of typical Cahors or Madiran, two wines of southwestern France.

[Pillow Talk

"You smell so sweet... sniff, sniff... it's driving me crazy!"

"That good?"

"Better!" he cried, throwing off his shyness – and his pyjamas. "A closer inspection is required, my beauty, but at first sniff, you smell like undergrowth after a spring shower! Drooping ferns, droplets of water trembling on velvet petals, the distilled essence of wintergreen blossoms... a nymph stirred by feeling, glowing with pleasure, inviting me to bite into her flesh and revel in her glorious tannins... .ah, my darling, what body!"

"Enough, already – cut the poetry! If you're looking for me, I'll be downstairs watching *The Sopranos*."

▌Should the poetical, impressionistic language of wine be taken seriously?

In the art of wine appreciation, as in most other arts, too much is as bad as too little. While the use of images and analogy is convenient and even desirable for describing a wine's character and for conveying our impressions, the hyperbole used in the past was off-putting for the uninitiated. Add to this an ingrained North American antipathy to flowery language, and you'll understand why the poetic tendencies of some wine writers tend to alienate the more pragmatic spirits among us. Take, for example, the expression used by the French, "cuisse de nymphe émue" (thigh of an emotionally stirred nymph), to describe a particular hue of rosé wine: it may well be included in *Larousse*, but it makes most of us smirk or roll our eyes.

Above all, highly coloured images should not be used to mask an inability to clearly and simply express what we think and feel about a wine.

Don't some aroma identifications require too much stretching of the imagination?

Not really. When certain wine writers claim that aromas of fresh paint, cannabis, or vinyl car-seats simply do not exist in wine, don't believe them.

At the risk of offending readers who are fond of universal truths, I can affirm that in the matter of smells, anything, or almost anything, is possible in wine tasting. Odours of paint, marijuana (close to that of new-mown hay), and vinyl are actually released by some wines. I've often been able to detect the presence of the American grape variety, Zinfandel, by a hint of vinyl in the wine. On the other hand, the fact that there are hundreds of different aromas in wine is not a justification to come up with examples that are too exotic or far-fetched.

If you are seriously striving to develop your wine-tasting ability, you should dare to advance your honest opinions in company, albeit modestly. For example, you might say: "I may be wrong, but don't you catch an aroma of mouldy cheese in this wine?" Only a sham wine connoisseur would retort that such an aroma does not exist in wine and that you, a neophyte, should take another sniff.

It goes without saying that differences of opinion largely depend on individual sensitivity to certain odours and flavours, and on each person's threshold of perception.

[Some Colourful Wine Expressions and Their Equivalents in Plain(er) English]

"This Syrah has a superb corsage."
> **for** "This Syrah is very fleshy."

"I adore virile wines."
> **for** "I adore very full-bodied wines."

"Ah, these wines that spread their peacocks' tails!"
> **for** "Wow! What a great finish!"

"Ingrid Bergman in red satin!"
> **for** "What silkiness!"

"This one has really got thighs!"
> **for** "Hard to imagine a fuller body."

"In my opinion, it's falling into lace."
> **for** "It's past its prime (has no more structure)."

"You'll have a cup of wine, won't you?"
> **for** "You'll have a glass of wine, won't you?"

"Give me a rising Gigondas."
> **for** "I like a heady style of Gigondas."

"Let's sabre the Champagne!"
> **for** "Let's uncork the Champagne!"

"A good wine, great sap!"
> **for** "A good wine, both rich and balanced."

Bingo!

"The ball is rolling, ladies and gentlemen. Give it another second... there! And the first aroma is: B-4, ambergris! The second lucky aroma... here it is! I-72, cloves! The third ball is rolling, and what have we got? N-24, Russian leather! Now for a duo – I see you're getting impatient, ladies and gentlemen. In sequence, then, and in a less refined register... ball four: G-56, sweat! And finally, ball number five: there you have it! O-22, bacon, good old Canadian bacon!"

"Bingo!" shouts a man at the back of the room, raising his glass of Hermitage.

No matter how I go about it, I can only detect one or two aromas in my glass of wine. Is there something wrong with me?

To answer this question, first let me quote, *in extenso*, from a wine book published in 1978 and addressed to novices(!):

"It is essential to unerringly recognize a certain number of odours, such as iris, hyacinth, rose, violet, mignonette, heather, apple, pear, peach, apricot, raspberry, cherry, wild cherry, banana, strawberry, bilberry, lemon, roasted almonds, cloves, vanilla, fern, new-mown hay, anise, mint, truffles, pine resin, basil, liquorice, sandalwood, juniper oil, toast, ambergris, musk, fur, game, venison, Russian leather, etc. And this is far from an exhaustive list."[2]

---

2. Fernand Woutaz, *Comment reconnaître 30 bons vins*, Hatier, 1978.

Even after many years as a professional taster and wine writer, I couldn't live up to this standard! Thus, if you find it difficult to identify the odours that you detect in wine, or have difficulty detecting them in the first place, this is no reason to be discouraged. Even the top experts in the field can rarely name more than three or four aromas in a particular wine. Moreover, tasters' comments are often very short and to the point. A typical example might be: "A fruity nose; cherry or raspberry aromas with a hint of vanilla; very drinkable."

There's nothing intimidating in that, is there? Yes, I admit, with experience, we can identify a greater number of aromas (scents, smells, odours, or whatever synonym you fancy). You can certainly develop your capacity to identify aromas by practising on food items or anything else that happens to be at hand. Before long – perhaps sooner than you expect – your efforts will bear fruit and you'll find yourself able to identify a wide range of aromas almost as soon as you detect them.

Here are two aide-mémoires to help you identify and categorize wine aromas. The first one lists particular aromas within the principal aroma categories found in wine. The second one shows which aromas are associated with the classic types of wine. Take a few moments to familiarize yourself with them before we return to the semantics of wine tasting.

[The Major Aroma Categories]

Small red fruits
└──● cherry, raspberry, strawberry, etc.

Small black-skinned fruits
└──● blackberry, black currant, black cherry, blueberry, etc.

Exotic or tropical fruits
└──● pineapple, mango, lychee, papaya, etc.

Other fruits
└──● banana, apple, orange, apricot, pear, grapefruit, dried fruits, etc.

Spices
└──● pepper, cinnamon, cloves, vanilla, nutmeg, etc.

Woody and toasted notes
└──● smoke, toast, chocolate, cocoa, coffee, cedar, spruce, caramel, etc.

Herbal and vegetal notes
└──● new-mown hay, dried grass, tobacco, green pepper, mushroom, eucalyptus, anise, etc.

Floral notes
└──● roses, violets, etc.

Sweet notes
└──● honey, candies, cookies, pastry, candied fruit, etc.

Noxious or disconcerting notes
└──● wet cardboard, damp basement, wet wool, rotten egg, sulphur, solvent, etc.

[Classic Wines and Their Characteristic Aromas]

Alsace

- Spruce gum (Riesling and Sylvaner), grapefruit (Riesling), and, when aged, honey and gasoline
- Rose, lychee, occasionally apricot (Gewürtraminer)

Red Bordeaux, Meritage® wines, Madiran, Cahors, etc.

- Black currant, green pepper, liquorice, cedar, newly turned earth, ink, red plums, cigar, pencil lead, mushrooms (Cabernet Sauvignon, Cabernet Franc, and Merlot)

Dry white Bordeaux and Loire Valley

- Cat's urine or boxwood (Sauvignon), honey (Sémillon and Chenin Blanc), anise

Sauternes and icewines

- Mango, celery, honey, beeswax, pineapple (Sémillon, Sauvignon, and Muscadelle); apricot, apple, lychee, melon, beeswax (Riesling, Vidal)

White Burgundy and New World Chardonnay

- Nuts, lemon, butter; caramel and smoke (very woody wines); wet wool (some Chablis wines; not a negative quality)

Red Burgundy and New World Pinot Noir

- Cherry, strawberry, rhubarb, cooked vegetables, animal or gamy notes, decomposing vegetation

Beaujolais
- Banana, bubblegum or candy aroma (called "English candies" by the French and "acid drops" by the English), strawberry

Red Rhône Valley and Languedoc
- Tobacco, cherry, and cinnamon (Grenache); olives, raw meat, bacon, smoke, and violets (Syrah); wild game, leather, and sweat (Mourvèdre)

Northern Italy
- Tar, cherries, and flowers (Nebbiolo)

Central Italy: Tuscany, Umbria, Veneto-Giulia
- Tobacco and cherries (Sangiovese)

Southern Italy
- Cherries, plums, and vinyl (Primitivo, Aglianico, etc.)

Spanish reds
- Raisins, vanilla, blackberries (Tempranillo)

Ruby port
- Floral notes, blackberry, black currant, and cherry (young ruby port); chocolate, cigars, and cedar (old ruby port)

Tawny port
- Fresh fruit: figs, oranges, plums and cherries (young tawny port); nuts, caramel, almonds, and brown sugar (old tawny port)

Besides these specific associations, you should also know that, generally speaking, the wine's colour indicates the aroma category you can expect to find in it. The fruitiness of white wine will practically never evoke red or black-skinned fruits, just as that of red wine will not evoke tropical fruits. All the other aroma categories, *grosso modo*, apply equally to reds and whites, as well as to rosés (which generally release aromas of red berries).

How precise should descriptions of the wine's bouquet be?

Saying "a fruity nose" when there is a distinct black currant aroma, or "floral notes" for an aroma that an experienced taster would identify as jasmine or lilac doesn't make much difference in the end.

After some time, however, if you've taken the trouble to practise smelling – singling out, recognizing and remembering individual odours – or if you're a conscientious cook or gardener, you'll probably want to be as precise as possible. Otherwise, very general terms or expressions are perfectly adequate for describing aromas in wine.

Thus, you'll often see the expression "red fruit" in the writings of wine critics, probably meaning that they can't quite decide if an aroma is strawberry and not raspberry, or even blackberry.

Is there a trick for detecting several aromas at once?

Try this: once you've identified one aroma, black cherry or black currant, for example, store it in your mind and take your nose and your attention away from your glass for a few seconds. Return to the attack, referring to the list of aroma categories if you like, and see if you can't single out another aroma or two, faint perhaps, or lurking in the background: something herbaceous, smoky, or spicy.

The Confessional

"Father, I have sinned. I was guilty of dishonesty again at a wine-tasting event, just last night. I told a bunch of lies. I made up aromas. I parrotted what the others said. I went to ridiculous lengths to avoid having to give my own opinion. I can't face myself anymore! I know that I've fallen from grace and have resolved to mend my ways. Give me any penance you see fit: I'm willing to do anything to get back on the straight and narrow path."

"Rise up, weak mortal! Your punishment shall be to get thyself to the wine store on Arthur Street... and save a place in the lineup for me! The Sassicaia has arrived!"

Honesty is said to be the best policy in wine tasting. How honest is honest?

Especially when you are a beginner at wine tasting, it's hard to come out and say frankly what you think of a particular wine. You might still lack confidence in your own judgment. You may be intimidated and afraid of sounding ridiculous, and therefore prefer to pass unnoticed rather than boldly express a potentially controversial point of view.

If another person, or, *a fortiori*, two or three other people, pronounce the wine you are drinking together "a dream," and you find that you can't work up the same enthusiasm, take the bull by the horns and express your difference of opinion as clearly as you can. Otherwise, you'll just have to play it cool by saying, "Sorry, but I don't find it so extraordinary. Maybe I'm just not getting the full taste," even if, in your heart, you know very well that your opinion is justified.

How does this honesty relate to the first impression?

If, when you first smell the wine in your glass, the word "flowers" immediately springs to mind, and if there isn't a vase of fresh-cut flowers on the table, or someone next to you who's doused with perfume or cologne, it must mean that the wine has a floral aroma. Otherwise, why would you have thought of flowers instead of nuts, or chocolate, for example? As far as the nose is concerned, always trust your first impression.

On the palate, it's a different matter: the first impression can be misleading. It's better to reserve judgment until the second mouthful. When tasting a tannic red wine with a "virgin" mouth – that is, when you haven't drunk or eaten anything just before – the wine may seem harsher and more aggressive than it would under other circumstances.

The corollary of the first impression on the nose, besides the fact that it is a precious tool when trying to identify a wine in a blind tasting, is that you should try not to be influenced by others around you if you want to keep your authentically personal opinion (this is where honesty comes in).

Of course, it's worthwhile pricking up your ears if there is an articulate, experienced wine taster in the vicinity, especially if you're lucky enough to be tasting the same wine. It will be reassuring to hear an expert corroborating your feeling that the wine is too astringent or too sweet. You'll also learn from comments such as: "It's the nature of this wine to be like that," because you'll know what to expect next time – and either get used to the characteristic in question, or know for sure that you don't like that wine and probably never will.

All of us, amateurs and professionals, are very easily influenced when tasting wine. It only takes one taster to suggest: "Don't you detect a hint of tar?" for the others to try the wine again and say: "You're right! Now that you mention it, it does have a tar undertone." I should emphasize that among seasoned tasters, we are constantly striving not to influence each other, although there are always a few incorrigibles who pronounce their verdict before the others have even looked at their glasses.

At the Airport

A large illuminated sign greets the disembarking travellers at the arrivals terminal:

Welcome! Nothing to declare? Turn left. All others, straight ahead.

"What's in this metal box here?"

"That?" said the traveller as the customs officer began unsealing the small case. "It's just a little specialty from back home. My mother," he explained, his voice breaking, "insisted that I take it with me."

"Pee-yew!" exclaimed the customs officer, recoiling from the open box. "What a stink! Baxter! Come over here a minute! No, no, we don't need the dog!"

"It's Corsican, Madame. It's a typical cheese from our valley. Niolo, it's called, and if I may say so, it has a wonderful smell!"

How can we say that wine smells of manure, cat's urine or decomposing vegetation, and still claim that it's good to drink?

In nature, all tastes have equal value. We know that one person can adore a smell that someone else finds abominable. This is also true in wine tasting – with the difference that, with experience, we get used to certain odours that we may have found repulsive at first, like sweat and decomposing leaves, and we even end up liking them.

Another reason that these bizarre aromas – which include the smells of the underside of a saddle and of gasoline – do not stop people from liking wine is that, in good wine, they mix with other, more agreeable aromas that possess at least some fruitiness. Thus, the overall bouquet and taste can be qualified as pleasant.

Aged red wines, especially old Burgundy, and most wines made from Mourvèdre grapes, exude animal notes. But this is a positive, sought-after characteristic, which is usually referred to as "gaminess."

I'm skeptical when I hear wine experts saying that wine smells like grapevine flowers, blackcurrant blossoms, civet or quince. How on earth can they pinpoint odours that are so far removed from their everyday lives?

While Europeans may be familiar with them, the smells mentioned above are practically non-existent in their natural state in North America – even that of the quince – and therefore, it is unlikely that we will recognize them in wine. However, we shouldn't necessarily be incredulous with respect to the astounding analogies used by certain wine critics in this hemisphere: they may have discovered these rare scents during a prolonged stay in Europe, or they may be Europeans who have migrated to these shores.

You can always fall back on wine-tasting kits made up of little vials of concentrated aromas (available in wine accessory stores) to practise smelling some of the more important odours that do not occur in nature here.

The ultimate consolation for us North Americans with regard to aroma detection is that the perfectly agreeable scents of spruce gum and maple syrup occasionally found in wine completely escape the notice of our cousins on the other side of the Atlantic.[3]

3. Maury and Banyuls, sweet wines from the south of France, often release an aroma of maple syrup. The odour of spruce gum is found in Alsatian Sylvaners and Rieslings, and certain white Mâcons.

[Section 3]
Serving Wine

The Power of Suggestion

"For best results, this red wine should be served at room temperature," urges the label on the back of bottle no. 1; the back label of
bottle no. 2 says: "Serve this elegant wine at 16-18°C (61-64 °F). The
label on bottle no. 3, on the other hand, contains no recommendations at all regarding the ideal drinking temperature of the wine, nor
any other serving suggestions.

At what temperature should wine be served? Does each type of wine have an ideal drinking temperature? Should I bother using a wine thermometer?

There is one simple answer to this multiple question: the vast
majority of white wines should be drunk chilled but not ice-
cold, and the vast majority of reds should be drunk cool, not
tepid or at room temperature.

More specifically, all whites, sparkling or still, dry or sweet,
should be served at approximately **7°C** (about 44°F). Since the
average refrigerator interior is about 5°C, a white wine will reach
its ideal temperature after about **three hours** of cooling. As for
reds, including dessert wines like ruby port, about an **hour and a
half** in the fridge will bring them to what is universally considered
the ideal temperature, that is, approximately **15°C** (about 60°F).
Since room temperature is commonly between 19 and 22°C (66-
72°F), bottles of red wine should always feel slightly cool to the
touch.

It's better to overdo it on the cold side and serve the wine a bit cooler than the ideal drinking temperature, rather than a degree or two warmer. Firstly, in the bottle and especially in the glass, cool wine will warm up to room temperature all too quickly in any case. Secondly, wine is more agreeable to drink when it refreshes the mouth and throat, not to mention that its fruity aromas and flavours are enhanced when it is relatively cool. When wine is tepid, it is mostly the alcohol rather than the fruit that rises to the nose when we try to assess the bouquet.

Lovers of nuance, note the following: the better the quality of the wine (this usually means more expensive), the warmer it can be served, without, however, exceeding the 18°C (65°F) limit. This rule extends to ordinary wines too: the poorer the quality of the wine (usually cheaper in price), the more it will gain by cooling. In the case of Beaujolais and other light, pale red wines, the temperature can even be lowered to 10°C (50°F).

If you're in a hurry, the bottle can be placed in an ice bucket, or better still in terms of convenience and speed, simply chilled in the freezer.

■ What? Wine in the *freezer*?

Yes! If this shocks your sensibilities, you should change your attitude. Most of the wine writers whom you read, emulate, and respect do precisely that.[1] Dinner is almost ready and that bottle of red Bordeaux is sitting on the sideboard or on the kitchen counter getting warmer every minute? Grab it and put it in the freezer, but – very important – don't forget to set the timer for fifteen minutes! If it's a white wine, its time in the freezer can be extended to thirty minutes.

1. Most Europeans, even those who have lived in North America for decades, will cringe at this suggestion. To them, it shows gross irreverence towards the sacred potion. No matter what irrefutable logical and factual arguments you give them, you'll never rid them of their conviction. It's a matter of culture, apparently.

Wine, an organic, living entity, is much more resilient and stable from a biochemical point of view than it is given credit for. In any case, immersing a bottle of wine in a cold liquid is more of a brutal shock than placing it in the cold air of the freezer, where heat loss occurs much less rapidly.

What should we do when wine is too cold – when a red wine has been in the refrigerator for days, for example?

Immersing the bottle in a container of warm water for a few minutes should be enough to bring the wine up to drinking temperature. It takes practice to get the timing right: if the bottle stays in too long, it will have to be put in the freezer for a few minutes afterwards! However, besides the inconvenience of these manipulations and in spite of objections from the would-be high priests of wine appreciation, this procedure does not diminish the wine in any way.

For an instant warm-up, can we use the microwave?

The heat in these ovens is created by microwaves causing the water molecules in food to vibrate, so perhaps we should be cautious where wine is concerned. Since about 85% of wine consists of water, it would be reckless indeed to affirm that microwave heating does not affect its balance or some other aspect of it. Nevertheless, in practice, it must be admitted that a glass of too-cold red wine does not seem to be adversely affected by spending a few seconds in the microwave oven at a low setting.

⌈Autopsy Report No.3489

The corpse was brought into the laboratory at noon. After an external examination revealed a rip in the label, the forensic toxicologist performed an incision in the cork to proceed with the analysis of the interior. A dull, brownish colour immediately indicated the direction that the probe should take, and clear signs of poisoning were quickly discovered. It was our conclusion that death had occurred less than 24 hours previously. No further investigation is necessary at this time, and no criminal charges will be laid. It has been established beyond the shadow of a doubt that the Ruchottes-Chambertin 1996 died from the effects of an oxygen overdose.

■ What should be done with leftover wine?

Once the bottle is open, the wine's worst enemy is the oxygen in the surrounding air. It has a period of grace of a few hours after uncorking, but when the meal is over, any wine left in the bottle should be dealt with right away before it succumbs to the effects of oxidation.

The ideal way to keep wine drinkable is to create a vacuum in the bottle, either with a mini-pump which extracts air by means of a valve in a rubber stopper, or a device which consists of a hollow plastic needle through which inert gas is injected from a spray can. Then, you just have to recork the bottle – if possible with the original cork, wine-soaked end downwards. In both methods, keep the bottle upright.

A half-empty bottle of wine can also simply be recorked and stored upright in the refrigerator, although it will not keep for more than one or two days.

None of these techniques, unfortunately, can prolong the wine's life for very long. The times that different types of wine can be preserved by these methods are presented on the following page. Note that my conclusions are based strictly on my own experience, not on scientific proof. Therefore, for safety's sake, my estimates are on the short side.[2]

If you know ahead of time that half a bottle will be enough for an occasion, you'll be ready to save the remainder. As soon as the bottle is open, pour the surplus quantity into a half-bottle that has been washed and rinsed. Cork it immediately. This way, the wine will last twice as long as it would have if left in the original bottle, even if it were vacuum-sealed or sprayed with inert gas.

Why do some wines seem to improve after staying in the uncorked bottle for a while?

This does happen, particularly in the case of very tannic reds or highly acidic whites. Oxidation, before it reaches the fatal stage, seems to give these wines a boost. They emerge more supple, softer, and less angular. Be aware, however, that this apparent improvement may work to the disadvantage of the aromas, which may begin to die away.

---

2. Alert readers may notice, among the above suggestions for conserving leftover wine, the absence of the simple method of freezing. This point has been given a special footnote for a purpose: to urge doubters to try it for themselves and to discover, prejudices aside, the procedure's effectiveness.

[Conservation Times for Opened Bottles]

(750-ml bottles)

	■ No protection; bottle half-full, simply recorked and placed in refrigerator	■ Same bottle, closed with vacuum pump, or sprayed with inert gas* *** The vacuum must be re-established, or the gas reapplied, after every use.**
Sparkling wine	12-24 hours	24 hours
Dry white wine	24-48 hours	4-5 days
Dry red and rosé	24 hours	3-4 days
Apéritif and dessert wine (icewines, Muscat, Pineau-des-Charentes, Sauternes, fino sherry, Marsala, etc.)	2-4 days	7 days
Red port (LBV, ruby, vintage)	3-5 days	7-10 days
Tawny port (10- and 20-year-old tawny, colheita)	20-25 days	25-30 days

[COMMENTS]

Sparkling Wine – Seal it with a special metal stopper or with a new cork, as the original cork swells up when removed. The disadvantage is that every time the bottle is opened and resealed, some of the carbon dioxide responsible for the effervescence escapes, and the wine loses its charm.

Dry white wine seems to resist oxidation better than red.

Dry red wine and rosé – Verify that the vacuum stopper is really airtight. You'll know if the contents are truly in a vacuum when you hear a slight pop on reopening the bottle.

Apéritif and dessert wine – Since most of these wines are known and enjoyed for their fruity aromas, they shouldn't be left for very long after opening. They will still be drinkable after the conservation limit that I've indicated in the table, but they will have lost much of their appeal for those who expect characteristic freshness and fruitiness.

Vintage port – In spite of its high alcohol content (20%), it rapidly loses its intense and captivating black fruit aromas once the bottle is begun.

Young tawny port will still taste good up to sixty days after opening. However, to an experienced palate, a noticeable decline sets in after about thirty days. Tawny port's long life is partly due to the fact that it is deliberately and heavily oxidized during its elaboration, and therefore needs less protection from the effects of air once it has been opened.

Elementary, my dear Watson?

The intentions are excellent and the advice as a whole judicious. It also tallies with what the majority of wine books say. Until recently, the following hint to consumers was still posted on the Internet site of the Quebec liquor commission:

"When several different bottles of wine are to be drunk at a dinner party, they should be served in ascending order of strength, as summarized by the following elementary rules:
– Dry white wine or rosé before red
– Chilled wine before wine at room temperature
– Light-bodied wine before full-bodied
– Dry wine before sweet
– Young wine before old
Keep in mind that the bottle of wine we are drinking should never make us regret the preceding one. Keep the best for the last!"

Elementary... really?

When several bottles of wine accompany a meal, which one should be opened first, and what determines the order?

Of the rules quoted above, the fundamental ones are "dry wine before sweet," and "the bottle of wine we are drinking should never make us regret the preceding one." If you can remember these two axioms, you'll be able to enjoy a combination of wines to the maximum, in most circumstances.

I certainly agree that it's a good idea to keep what is presumed to be the best wine of the evening for the last, building up a crescendo in your tasting enjoyment as you go along. On the other hand, the dinner can be orchestrated in another tempo altogether, with two different wines being served simultaneously, stimulating the drinkers to informally discuss the respective merits of the two. The advantage of the second strategy is that there is less chance that people's palates will be exhausted by the time the best wine of the evening is served. Of course, in both of the above scenarios, a little restraint is needed so that the best wines won't be treated as quaffing wines and thoughtlessly chugged down.

The dry-before-sweet rule is also fundamental. Avoid serving icewine, Muscat, or Sauternes as an apéritif before drinking good dry red wines. The sugar in the sweet wine coats the tongue and permeates the taste buds, with the result that the red wine drunk afterwards will seem thin and acidic.

In contrast, dry white wine – sparkling or still – possesses the happy quality of quickening the appetite and preparing the terrain for the arrival of the reds. Some people find its lively acidity overwhelming, but they should know that it doesn't take much practice to become used to it and even to enjoy it. A bite of food will counterbalance the acidic factor, for those who find it too abrasive. Otherwise, they could try dry white wine from California, Canada or Australia as a preprandial stimulant: many of these New World whites are rich and fat, even velvety, when they have been aged in wood.

Note that it's quite acceptable to follow a red by a dry white wine which may be more compatible with cheese at the end of the meal. Loire Valley whites and New World Chenins are supremely suitable for this purpose.

Radio Forum

"On *Wine Debate* today, we have one hot topic on the agenda: Should wine be allowed to breathe before serving? We've got two experts with us in the studio, a biochemist and a poet, who are going to defend their opposing points of view. I can tell you, after talking with them earlier, that it's going to be one hell of a programme, pardon my language. You too can have your say, by calling... "

▌Should wine be allowed to "breathe" before being served?

I n 98% of cases, no. Almost all the ordinary wines consumed at home, in the less-than-$20-a-bottle category, should just be cooled slightly, uncorked and drunk with no further ado.

If some wines do improve by a little ventilation after being confined for most of their lives in their airless glass prisons, it would be an illusion to think that the small amount of air that can pass through a narrow bottleneck will make much difference. To "breathe" properly, the wine must be decanted into a carafe. This does, in effect, aerate the wine, and may produce an impression of greater balance and smoothness, as if the wine had undergone an accelerated aging process.

⌈The First Day of School

"Welcome to Wine Tasting 405, the final course in your master's programme. We'll start by making sure everyone has the appropriate class materials. Starting next week, you will not be allowed back in the seminar room unless you have your complete set of wine glasses with you, beginning with your stainless steel thimble... joke! Seriously, you must have all of the following: one sherry *copita*, one Alsatian green-stem, one tulip glass, two Burgundy 'bowls,' one Bordeaux glass, one Impitoyable No. 5, one Riedel Vinum ice-wine glass, one standard Inao glass, one port glass... "

What is the best kind of glass for drinking wine?

I f you want to choose a single type of wine glass that will be more than adequate for your initiation period, the best one is without a doubt the Inao glass. Its name derives from the Institut National des Appellations d'Origine, the French wine standards organization that contributed to its design and manufacture in the 1970s. It is sold in wine accessory stores. Buy the lightest and finest type of crystal Inao glass. These are made in France, Italy, and the Czech Republic.

If you can't find the authentic Inao, use a glass that has the same basic characteristics. It should be at least a 250-ml (8-ounce) stem glass, with a plain surface (not cut, engraved or textured on the outside) and a convex opening (narrower at the top than in the middle). If your glass is not properly shaped (as close to egg-shaped as possible), it will be much harder to smell the wine's aromas: they will literally deflect to either side of your nose. Any glass that fulfils the above criteria will be appropriate for all types of wine, from sparkling wine to port. That said, the Champagne *flûte* (not the *coupe*, which is far too wide at the mouth) will always be a becoming addition to your glassware.

When you are sure that your interest in wine is not just a passing fancy, you may want to graduate to another kind of glass, one that functions just as well, but is slimmer and more elegant, with a longer stem.

There is a wide choice (and a corresponding wide range of prices) in this more refined make of wine glass. The Overture series made by the Austrian company, Riedel, and the Oenologue series made by the French company, Cristal d'Arques, are particularly good; any self-respecting wine lover should own at least six of one type or the other. After you've tried drinking wine in these glasses, you'll agree that the $100 or so could not have been better spent.

Why have I seen people smelling their empty glasses just before the wine is poured?

Even on those exclusive gourmet food-and-wine events that draw crowds of experts on Brillat-Savarin and first growths, it happens – and happens surprisingly often – that the wine glasses, even if they are made by Riedel or Spiegelau, smell funny. To drink wine to its best advantage, the glass must be perfectly neutral from the equally important points of view of colour, texture, and odour. The most common odour found malingering in wine glasses is that of rag or dishcloth. Wine glasses also occasionally smell of cardboard or dust, as if they had stayed too long in their packing boxes.

At home, a common error is to store glasses upside-down on the shelf. Any odour in the cupboard – the smell of closed air, cooking, or even paint – will be trapped inside the glass, and must be gotten rid of before wine is poured into it.

When you're setting the table for dinner guests, quickly sniff one or two of your wine glasses. If you detect an odour, pour a little wine into one glass and swirl it around until the wine has coated all of the inside. Pour the remains into the next glass, and repeat the procedure until all your glasses have been "seasoned," or "baptized," as the Italians say.

After this operation, although the glasses may not be absolutely neutral, they'll be well-primed to carry out their function.

Checking the glasses, and seasoning them if necessary, may seem overly fastidious at first, but it will become second nature to you after you have done it a few times.

How full should the glass be?

Never more than half full; ideally, a third-full. This allows you to give the wine a good swirl so that it can release its aromas. A modest portion in every glass also means that whenever a new bottle arrives on the table, it will be distributed more evenly among the people present, and they will have an equal chance to enjoy each wine as it is opened. Apart from that, not everyone knows how to swirl wine properly, and just the presence of a larger amount of air in the glass encourages the aromas to rise.

No matter which type of glass you are using, hold it by the stem, or even by the base, if you prefer. This is not a question of table manners: if you hold the bowl of the glass in your hand, the wine will warm up, and some of its aromas and flavours will be diminished. As I stress repeatedly in this book, red wine should be drunk cool, not tepid or at room temperature!

Should we use a clean glass when we change wines?

Unless your glass is covered with greasy finger-marks or lipstick smudges, it can be used continuously throughout the meal when several different wines are served in succession.

Besides making sure that your glass is empty before accepting a different wine, you can "season" it with a little of the new wine before the customary amount is poured. Naturally, pouring a dessert wine (Sauternes or icewine, for example) into a glass that has held a dry red will not enhance it. In this case, it's better to wash or change the glass.

As for drinking particular types of wine in differently shaped glasses, the Inao, Overture, and Oenologue are a good fit for all types; there is no need to use several glasses during a multi-wine occasion.

Haven't wine glasses made by Riedel, Crystal d'Arques, etc., become the norm these days, supplanting the Inao glass?

Some status-conscious wine lovers have started to look askance at the Inao glass. Also, at the more prestigious wine-tasting events, this trusty glassware is no longer the standard. This development should not necessarily be a matter for regret: the Inao, comparatively heavy and squat, has been surpassed by finer, more beautiful glassware.

On the other hand, no serious studies have ever succeeded in demonstrating the sensory superiority of the taller, supposedly more specialized glasses. In fact, they are running nose to nose with the Inao in this unofficial contest, at least for the time being. Researchers at the Université de Bordeaux compared the performances of three makes of wine glass, using a fine Spanish wine (a 1996 Vega-Sicilia Valbuena) as test material. They reported that: "the Inao glass gave off the highest concentration of aromas. In particular, it presented more hyacinth, pear, and rose-petal scents than the Grand Jury Européen glass" (almost identical to a Riedel Overture glass).[3]

A footnote to this experiment is that the aromas (in their volatile or gaseous state) were measured by chromatography. In other words, instead of fallible, subjective human perception, a scientific instrument detected and analyzed the aroma molecules that emerged from the glass – the rose-petal aroma corresponding to the geraniol molecule, the pear aroma to the hexyl acetate molecule, etc.

It is true that the flesh-and-blood wine taster raising a glass to drink can be favourably predisposed towards its contents by the vessel's very elegance. He or she may sincerely find that the wine tastes better in fine stemware, and may forsake the Inao glass in consequence. This is quite natural, and it is perhaps even preferable that an element of human emotion be allowed to temper rigid scientific objectivity in this area.

---

3. *Sciences et Avenir*, special edition, No. 120.

■ Can wine glasses be put in the dishwasher?

They shouldn't, unless you run the cycle without soap, using very hot water. White chalky residue may accumulate on glassware washed in an automatic dishwasher. Besides that, most detergents are abrasive and may dull or even scratch fine crystal.

You can wash the glasses in the sink with ordinary dishwashing liquid, but be careful to rinse them well in hot water before letting them dry. Or, better still, dry them with a no-lint cloth.

The glasses must be impeccable when they are set on the table, that is, spotless and odourless – totally neutral and ready to play their role of presenting the wine to its best advantage.

[Screwing Around

"I use the Swiss piston model: it never fails."

"The one with the double camshaft at the top?"

"Stop making fun of me!"

"Admit it, it's ridiculous – all this sophisticated technology just to get a piece of cork out of a bottle."

"You've obviously never had to struggle with a really tight cork!"

■ Is the type of corkscrew important?

It is, although a variety of models do a good job. Avoid, whenever possible, corkscrews with shafts (called "worms") that are not helical (open in the centre, like pigs' tails). A corkscrew with a solid shaft like a drill – basically, a screw – may shred the cork, especially in bottles of a certain age, or that have been standing upright for a long time. This type of corkscrew spears right through the cork instead of winding more delicately and evenly through it by a spiral route. Then, when the levers are pushed down, instead of pulling the cork out of the bottle, the solid shaft may tear upward through it, breaking it into pieces and leaving part of it in the bottle neck.

The classic waiter's corkscrew or the double-lever Pulltaps (which both have helical worms) are adequate for most bottle-opening situations. The better-quality models are sold in wine stores. The more luxurious models of corkscrew – Screwpull or Trudeau, for example – are a pleasure to use, but you can get along well enough without them.

Is there is proper technique for opening the bottle?

Yes. First, trim off the top of the capsule (the metallic or plastic cover), cutting it just under the rim of the bottle neck. If your corkscrew doesn't have the little accessory blade for this, remove the whole capsule. This is done so that the wine will pour freely from the bottle, without coming into contact with a jagged-edged or soiled capsule.

Place the point of the corkscrew worm in the centre of the (clean) cork top and start screwing downwards, trying to keep it straight and well-centred. If the worm deviates (gets too close to the glass of the bottle's neck), don't persist: unscrew the corkscrew and start over.

■ What about opening Champagne?

Contrary to the tradition at the end of a Formula One car race, the main idea is to conserve the effervescence – all those lovely bubbles that so much time and effort have gone into creating inside the bottle, especially in the case of Champagne.

Remove the foil and the wire cage that holds the cork in place, carefully, so that there's no danger of it popping out too soon. Another precaution: make sure that you're not pointing the bottle in the direction of a fellow living creature or a breakable object, for obvious reasons.

Tilt the bottle at a 45-degree angle, holding it by the base in one hand. Grip the cork firmly in the other hand, then turn the bottle by the base. If this manoeuvre is successful, you'll hear a discreet "psssh" as the cork eases out of the bottle neck while you continue to hold it firmly.

Do bits of floating cork mean that the wine is defective?

No, it doesn't mean that the wine has cork taint. You can remove the debris by tilting your glass and fishing it out with a piece of cutlery, and nothing more need be said about it. Almost all of the cork particles will probably go into the first glass poured, which, as a polite host or hostess, you will put aside for yourself.

Flowers Last Longer

"Red alert! Red alert!"

"What's going on?"

"We're invited to my sister's for dinner on Thursday."

"Uh-oh. What are we supposed to bring?"

"Wine! Can you believe it?"

"Ah, no! We decided never again! Hors d'oeuvres, dessert, bread, cheese, pizza for the kids, anything but wine! Last time, we spent hours choosing a bottle good enough for them!"

What do you do when you're invited to dinner by a wine connoisseur, or when you're having one over for dinner?

There's no need to panic. When you're the invitee, it's a good idea to ask about the dinner fare, in relation to the wine that you propose to bring. The redoubtable but not unapproachable wine connoisseur will be pleased that you're asking for his or her advice. You might say, for instance: "I'd like to bring a white wine to go with the entrée if that's all right with you. What type do you think I should be looking for?" Or, if the party is at your house, tell the expert what the menu will be and ask for advice in the same manner.

All you have to do after that is head for the wine store or liquor commission and find one or another bottle of the suggested category. And if you truly value the connoisseur's friendship, you'll spend a bit more than the $15 that you usually pay for your Saturday evening bottle of wine. Go up a notch to the $20-$25 range: your friend will appreciate the evidence that you have gone to a little extra trouble to mark the occasion.

Another way to avoid a fiasco is to entrust the purchasing of the bottles for the evening to the person who's most in the know about wine. Thus: "There are going to be six of us on Friday night. I talked with the others, and, if its okay with you, we're each going to contribute $15 towards the wine. That makes $90 for you to play with, that is, if you think it's enough…"

The chosen wine consultant, being a good friend, will gladly go along with this plan. And on the evening in question, don't be surprised if he or she has gone beyond the call of duty and has graciously added a special wine, outside the allotted budget.

Going Over the Books

"What's this item here in non-reimbursable deductions? $50 for a decanter?"

"It's an office expense, Pauline, office equipment."

"And if you get audited, do you think you can prove that this item of 'office equipment' is necessary to generate business?"

"Send me an auditor who's remotely human, at lunchtime any day of the week, and for a minor fee, I'll give them a crash course in decanting and wine tasting, my style!"

"Yes, but... "

■ How should a decanter be used?

Take the decanter out of mothballs and dust it off. Almost everyone owns at least one decanter that they received as a gift or inherited; usually it's taking up space at the back of a cupboard or sitting, decorative but unused, on a shelf.

Like wine glasses, the decanter, preferably a crystal one, should be clean and free of any impurities. Rinse it and season it with wine before filling it.

Wine is decanted – poured into a carafe – for two main reasons: to aerate it and to make it look beautiful. In the past, wine was decanted to get rid of sediment, inoffensive but unattractive, by leaving it behind in the original bottle. This is rarely necessary today, except in the case of certain vintage ports, old wine

(20-30 years old), and the occasional unfiltered or partially filtered vintage.

When a red wine, or sometimes even a white, is mute in terms of aroma and taste, and you have good reason to believe that this is because the wine is too young or has not been sufficiently aged in the bottle, pouring it into a decanter may make a difference, recreating some of the positive effects of aging.

In a wide-bottomed decanter, the surface of the wine in contact with the air is much greater than in a wine bottle. A beneficial oxygenation may occur with airing, which contributes, in the case of red wine, to softening and rounding out tannins that may have been too firm and harsh at first. However, you should at least taste the wine before deciding that it might improve by decanting.[4]

The great advantage of using a decanter is that it shows off the beauty of the wine's robe (colour). It also creates an elegant atmosphere at a meal, even when the wine would have tasted just as good if it had been served directly from the bottle.

Always place the original bottle on the table so your guests can see for themselves what they're drinking and can look at the front and back labels if they want more details.

■ What if you don't have a decanter handy?

You can still decant and aerate wine by transferring it from its original bottle to another bottle or other vessel that has been washed and carefully rinsed. Use a little of the wine to season the other recipient. After emptying it, pour the rest of the wine into it, then back into the original bottle by means of a plastic funnel kept exclusively for this purpose. You can do this a couple of times if you think the wine needs a really good airing.

---

4. Some wine buffs don't think twice before decanting the contents of a bottle of wine, old or young, that has just been opened at home or at a restaurant. Their view – a defensible one – is that the wine cannot lose by it, and might gain something.

■ Can wine be preserved in a decanter?

Generally speaking, no – or rather, if the stopper is airtight, for twelve hours at the most. The exception is a wine that has already been oxidized – old tawny port, for example. However, studies have shown that when wine remains in a crystal decanter for a prolonged period of time, the crystal eventually releases toxic lead particles.

▮ How can we clean a decanter that is stained on the inside?

There is no definitive solution when this happens. Many different techniques have been recommended – rinsing with coarse salt and vinegar, with grains of rice in water, or with crushed egg shells in water, to name only a few. The idea is to shake one of these mixtures inside the decanter to scrape the stains off (these are usually quite stubborn and encrusted, as decanters are often used for full-bodied, dark-coloured wines, or highly concentrated ports).

These formulae work, up to a point. The winning combination is white vinegar and a quarter-cup of rice. The booby prize is that, after cleaning, the carafe may be clear and bright, but an indelible purplish tint remains. Of course, when the decanter is filled again with red wine, this is not a problem – as long as you accept that henceforth, its use will be restricted to wine of that colour.

■ What is the proper way to dry a decanter?

The ideal way is to use a special bottle drainer or drying rack, or to improvise one. The "Christmas tree" bottle-drying stand, used by home wine makers who must clean and prepare a large number of bottles for siphoning, is excellent: the bottles dry upside-down and the runoff is collected in a basin at the bottom of the stand. Narrow, elongated carafes will dry well on the tree.

Otherwise, it gets a bit complicated. Care must be taken not to leave water inside the decanter, as it will stagnate and stink. Some people have told me that they use a twisted piece of paper towel as a wick, letting it down to the bottom of the decanter, where it will absorb any remaining wetness. Obviously, the top end of the wick would have to emerge far enough out of the bottle neck for this method to be effective. Not having tried it myself, I am reserving judgment for the moment.

[Section 4]

Food and Wine Harmony

Hold the Curry, Chef!

"How many times do I have to tell you? You *know* how much I hate it when someone's looking over my shoulder while I'm cooking!"

"Calm down – I just want to know if you're still intending to use fresh coriander in the sauce."

"And *I* just have to say it again: I don't know yet! I'll decide when I do the sauce, and that's that!"

"My reason for asking is that I was going to open a bottle of La Mouline."

"Why didn't you say so? What year?"

"Nineteen ninety-six, the year we tasted it in the cask at Guigal's in Ampuis."

"All *right*! Put the coriander back in the fridge for me and get out the pressed duck, baby!"

What are the general rules regarding food and wine combinations?

There are two main points of view on the subject, two different, and in a sense, opposing approaches. In one, wine is sovereign and gastronomy must bow to it, while in the other – what we might refer to as a shotgun wedding – the food and the wine are thrown together and are forced to try to get along.

In the first approach, the wine is the lead-off and the menu is chosen to complement it. The food must be good but not too spicy or salty, or with too much vinegar in it. To do the honours to a great red wine – a bottle of Hermitage, for example – the meal could consist of a leg of lamb, duck, or plain roast beef. It might be the ultimate mistake to drink the Hermitage with a California-style medley, which is more often "confusion" than "fusion" cuisine. With this kind of wild menu, the wine would have a very hard time expressing itself, and the food would overwhelm it. Aromas, taste, nuances, suppleness: none of the wine's trumps would be played. The great Hermitage would still taste like wine, but like ordinary wine.

If you appreciate good wine even a little and respect the incredible care that goes into its elaboration, you'll agree that putting it at risk of having its flavours cancelled out is a sacrilege.

But isn't wine meant to be drunk while eating?

Certainly! But this shouldn't prevent us from bringing out its good points and making it the centre of attention every once in a while. This doesn't necessarily mean spending a lot of time searching for the perfect or ideal match, which is, in the end, more of a philosophical question than anything else, with nothing exact or objective about it.

Subjugating the food to the wine seems reasonable. What about the shotgun wedding approach?

Fine wine is often an unwilling partner when we insist on marrying it to dishes as impressive as itself, or to food which may be delicious and expertly prepared, but which packs an overdose of flavours. Having experienced it myself on many occasions (often with other wine specialists who were as disappointed as I was) by the turn of events), I have learned that the "great food for a great wine" policy, in spite of the best of intentions and the most scrupulous planning and execution, almost always fails to achieve its goal and results in a denial of justice for the wine.

The fare that accompanies a very good wine should be succulent, yet simple and unpretentious. This does not imply that the food should be dull: far from it! We can take our inspiration from Luc de Conti, owner of the Château La Tour des Gendres in Bergerac (north of Bordeaux), on the best way to serve fresh truffles: "As in all classic dishes, the preparation should be simple: hot toast with a dribble of olive oil and the sliced truffles on top, *au naturel.*"

So it should be between a great wine and the food chosen to give it its place in the sun.

Fine wines with classic dishes are great for connoisseurs, but what about us common mortals? What type of wine goes with fish, for example?

I won't pretend that there's any mystery to that: white, obviously – dry and lively if possible, with a good amount of acidity. White wines from the Loire Valley – Pouilly-Fumé and Sancerre – are excellent with fish and seafood. There is a huge range of choice as far as regions and countries are concerned. In Italy alone, you'll find many white wines that are excellent with fish – from Piedmont in the north to Sicily in the south. In reality, almost all white wines are suitable.

There are exceptions to this rule. Fish that are fatty or oily, or have red or pink flesh (eg., salmon, tuna, or swordfish) also go well with light-bodied reds, low in tannins, like some Burgundies, New World Cabernets Francs, and, again, some wines from the Loire Valley (Chinon, Bourgueil, and Saumur-Champigny). Rosé, if you like it, is also good, as long as it is dry enough; this may be hard to determine, as it's not marked on the label. You can, however, have a good idea of a rosé's relative dryness by its alcohol content: high usually means dry, with the driest rosés reaching a 13% or even a 13.5% alcohol rate.

■ What about wine with meat?

This is also fairly straightforward, since almost any red wine will go with meat. The darker the meat, the more full-bodied and deeply coloured the wine should be. The aromas and flavours of a light-bodied Beaujolais will be overwhelmed by the dark meat of wild game (venison, pheasant, etc.). The inverse is also true: the paler the meat (veal, pork, chicken, etc.), the lighter-bodied the wine should be. Richer, more strongly flavoured whites – New World wines being a notable example – accompany white meat very well.

■ And with cheese?

Contrary to what is frequently said and written, cheese is hostile to wine. This is particularly true of fine red wines: the cheese almost always obliterates their personality. Nonetheless, the pairing of wine and cheese is still synonymous with perfect harmony. These two are the world's most legendary couple after Romeo and Juliet! You only have to think of the number of wine-and-cheese parties held on almost every occasion imaginable. The average wine-and-cheese table is not usually orchestrated to be a gourmet's delight: more likely, it is an easy, inexpensive way to accommodate the maximum number of people at a convivial get-together (often for fund-raising purposes).

If wine absolutely must accompany cheese, start with red wine for the pâté and cold cuts, and serve the cheese afterwards with white wine. The type of white wine for drinking with cheese is basically the same as for fish: dry and lively.[1] Because of its acidity and lack of tannin, white wine is less likely to be undermined by the powerful odours and flavours of cheese than red is. Note, however, that the vanilla flavours of oak-aged New World whites (e.g., California Chardonnays) do not always blend well with cheese.

On the other hand, some regional combinations, that is, wines and cheeses traditionally made in close proximity, are justifiably famous. Some examples are: Alsatian Munster washed down with local Gewurztraminer, Swiss raclette with Fendant (Valais), Crottin de Chavignol with Sancerre (Loire), and Gorgonzola with Amarone.[2] Other famous combinations are consecrated by long tradition, for example, Stilton and port.[3]

At home, dessert wines, fortified or not, can be drunk with cheese at the end of a meal. Thus, blue cheese and even goat's or sheep's cheese, can be nibbled with Sauternes, Muscat, icewine, Madeira, or port.

■ What should be drunk with dessert?

Would it be offensive to suggest a good cup of coffee? Certainly not dry red, white, or rosé wine. There should be an answering sweetness in the accompanying

1. White wine can perfectly well follow red, either at professional wine tastings or at the dinner table. At the top tasting events of Bordeaux, where dozen of reds and whites are assessed at random, reds are customarily presented before whites, which possess the happy ability to refresh the tasters' weary palates.
2. The town of Gorgonzola (near Milan) is about 150 km. west of Verona, where Amarone is made; thus, the concept of region is a bit broader than for the other combinations mentioned here.
3. To be sure, Stilton is made in England and port in Portugal, but there is an undeniable English facet to port, since it was developed mainly by the British in the seventeenth century and is still associated with them, as seen in the names of major producers Taylor, Graham, Cockburn, etc.

beverage – not too much, however, or the sugar in both elements of the combination will make them seem sickly sweet.

To give your taste buds a fighting chance to appreciate a good dessert wine, drink it before you bite into the dessert, or after you have finished the food, savouring the wine as you would a liqueur.

If you like to serve sparkling wine as a grand finale to a dinner party, choose a slightly sweet one. In the case of Champagne, it is the misleading "Extra-Dry" on the label that identifies it as semi-sweet.

▋ Are there any absolute taboos – combinations that should be avoided at all costs?

Wine should never be drunk with salad, nor with hot soup. The vinegar in most salad dressings and the heat of soups are incompatible with wine in the mouth, the shock occurring on the taste level in the first case, and on the thermal level in the second. Recuperate by drinking water and chewing a piece of bread. Watch out, too, for raw garlic, marinated raw fish, anchovies (truly catastrophic), and sushi condiments (horseradish and pickled ginger), all of which are capable of knocking out the hardiest wines.

▋ Are the classic wine and food matches still the thing these days?

They are, even more so than in the past. With the explosion of new cooking philosophies and techniques and the current fascination with world cuisine, cooking styles seem to be heading in various directions at once these days. It is therefore reassuring to fall back on time-tested values, especially since the most renowned traditional combinations, based on long experience, have the merit of bringing out the best in both the wine and the food. Besides the wine and cheese marriages mentioned above, some of the most famous matches are:

- lamb with Bordeaux
- oysters with Chablis or Muscadet
- roast chicken with Beaujolais
- almonds or hazelnuts with dry sherry (fino or manzanilla)
- cassoulet with red wine from the south of France (Cahors, Madiran, Buzet)
- bouillabaisse with Bandol
- sauerkraut with Sylvaner
- paella with Rioja rosé
- foie gras with Sauternes
- beef with Côtes-du-Rhône
- asparagus with dry Alsatian Muscat (or Argentine Torrontés)

How can you objectively measure the relative success or failure of a food-and-wine combo?

It will be clear that the marriage works if, after a few mouthfuls of both the food and the wine, each one continues to taste as good as it did at the start. Ideally, each of the partners will accommodate the other without denying themselves or becoming embittered. It may not always be the most romantic or passionate union, but it is still a partnership if the food and wine both taste very good without one overshadowing the other, or without the two of them mutually diminishing each other.

Isn't a compatible marriage between food and wine supposed to produce absolute bliss, perfection – something far beyond the sum of their respective parts?

This does happen, but very rarely, and usually only after extensive trial and error. Even then, the equation is almost always skewed on one side or another – besides being practically impossible to achieve more than once. There are too many variables involved: cooking times, type of sauce, spices and herbs used (that aromatic but jarring fresh coriander!), the choice of vegetables to accompany the meat or fish, etc.

This is why a classic, simple dish has a much better chance of achieving harmony with a great wine.

Food and Wine Marriages

[Important: never more than lightly salted or seasoned]

■ Hors d'oeuvres

CONVENTIONAL COMBINATIONS

- Any kind of sparkling wine
- Almost any kind of dry white wine
- Apéritif wine (Pineau-des-Charentes, Muscat de Beaumes-de-Venise, bitter vermouth)

Comments: Avoid ouzo, arak, raki, pastis, or any other anise-based liquor: their strong aftertaste will annihilate your wine-tasting ability for some time. A good *apéritif typique* is Lillet Blanc from Bordeaux – light, fruity, and refreshing.

MORE DARING MATCHES

- Sherry (manzanilla or fino)
- White port

Comments: Manzanilla and fino sherries are so dry that they almost feel like dust in the mouth. You should drink them every so often to get accustomed to them, as they go wonderfully well with hors d'oeuvres. White port is sweet, sometimes cloyingly so. Its syrupy texture will coat the tongue and remain inlaid in it, so to speak. As with sweet Muscat, refrain from drinking it when good dry red wine is to follow.

■ Hot soups and salads with vinegar in the dressing

- Water

■ Fish

CONVENTIONAL COMBINATIONS

- Almost all dry whites as long as they're not too woody. The best are lively with a noticeable acidity
- Rosé with pink-fleshed trout

MORE DARING MATCHES

- Light-bodied reds, low in tannins, for grilled fatty fish like salmon, tuna, or swordfish
- Semi-sweet whites for rich and creamy sauces

■ Shellfish

CONVENTIONAL COMBINATIONS

- Muscadet, Riesling, or Chablis with oysters
- Full-bodied Chardonnay, lightly oaked, with lobster and crab
- Riesling and Graves (Bordeaux) whites with scallops, clams, and shrimps

MORE DARING MATCHES

- Sauternes and lobster
- Sauternes and oysters
- Light-bodied (Beaujolais-type) reds with oysters

■ Poultry and other white meat
– including sweetbreads, tripe, etc.

CONVENTIONAL COMBINATIONS

- Medium- or light-bodied reds, deep-tinted rosés
- Whites that are not very lively or crisp: Bordeaux, Pinot Gris, Chardonnay with chicken livers
- Fairly acidic, tannic reds (e.g., Chianti) with osso bucco

MORE DARING MATCHES

- Semi-sweet or sweet white wine with chicken in a tropical fruit sauce

■ Red meat
– including liver, sausages, etc.

CONVENTIONAL COMBINATIONS

- Almost all kinds of red wine, with full-bodied and robust reds for strongly flavoured dark meat (wild game)
- Full-bodied and tannic reds with beef stew or braised beef

Comment: When serving highly tannic wine, it is recommended to serve the (grilled or roasted) meat rare to temper possible harshness.

MORE DARING MATCHES

- Strong rosés with roast beef
- New World rosés with veal liver
- Pinot Gris or white Rhône with steak tartare

■ Cheese

- White or red wine (the latter generally goes better with hard cheese)
- Dessert wines with blue cheese

MORE DARING MATCHES

- Dessert wines (e.g., Jurançon, Loire Valley, German late-harvest whites) with Swiss raclette

Comments: No great red wine should be drunk with any type of cheese whatsoever. If this situation arises, at least avoid eating the cheese rinds to minimize the damage. Avoid white wines aged in oak: vanilla notes often clash with cheese.

■ Desserts

CONVENTIONAL COMBINATIONS

- Dessert wines
- Tawny port or Banyuls with chocolate

MORE DARING MATCHES

- Good coffee with chocolate

Comment: Watch out for chocolate that is labelled pure: if it is 80% cacao or more, it will overwhelm any wine.

[World Food and Wine]

H ere, the approach is different, with the choice of wine depending on the style of cooking. Only the more exotic cuisines are included below: when we are dealing with French, Italian, Spanish, or Portuguese cooking, we can easily stay within the well-known national or regional wine-and-food matches.

North African and Middle Eastern
- Rich and full-bodied reds and whites
- Light acidic white wines, rosés, and beer, to offset strong spices and to quench the thirst

Chinese, Japanese, and Korean
- Dry or semi-sweet whites – Alsatian Gentil, Argentine Torrontés, Gewurztraminer, etc.
- New World reds (Chilean or California Merlot)
- Fairly rich Vouvray-type sparkling whites

Thai, Khmer, and Vietnamese
- Dry or semi-sweet whites
- Still or sparkling cider
- Spiced beer, refermented in the bottle

Indian and Mexican
- Alsatian or German whites
- California Zinfandel
- Amarone
- Young LBV port, or ten-year-old tawny port, chilled
- Porter, or dark Canadian microbrewery beers

Eastern European

- Light-bodied Gamay-type reds (Loire Valley, Beaujolais, Valpolicella, etc.)
- Rustic, robust reds (Bulgarian, Slovenian, Rumanian, etc.)

Greek

- Whites, including retsina
- Rosés (Rosé de Provence, for example)
- Light and acidic reds (Gamay, Beaujolais, Sangiovese, etc.)

[Section 5]
Drinking Wine in Restaurants

Business Lunch Bust

It was one of those days. The subcontractor who was supposed to make a delivery first thing in the morning still hadn't shown up by noon. The meeting scheduled for the reorganization of the company was cancelled, for the third time! Then they called from the daycare centre to say that Junior had pulled little Chelsea Wong's hair again...

This disaster scenario spilled over to my lunch appointment with two of our biggest clients, who, for some reason, were in a cantankerous mood. When they rejected the third bottle of wine in a row, the waiter, obviously about to explode, turned on his heel and started walking off. Without turning around, he snapped: "Nobody move! I'm going to get the sommelier!"

Should we follow the sommelier's advice at a restaurant?

We should. Although many of them are a bit pretentious, most professional sommeliers (sometimes referred to as wine stewards) have studied their subject and have a degree in wine purchasing and cellar management from a technical school, college, or specialized institution (e.g., the Court of Master Sommeliers in London, England). If they are employed at a reputable restaurant, they must have a good knowledge, not only of the wines listed, but of the menu items as well.

Therefore, on the whole, yes, we should follow the sommelier's suggestions regarding combinations from the *carte des vins* and the *table d'hôte*, just as we should respect his or her verdict on the wine bottles brought to the table.

If there seems to be something wrong with the wine recommended by the sommelier – if it tastes strange or not at all like I expected – what should I do?

Sommeliers are not infallible, but if they are conscientious and are authorized by the restaurant to express their honest opinions, then they will tell you frankly, after tasting the wine, if you are right or wrong to suspect that something is amiss. Perhaps, if the wine is not corked, or faulty in some other way, the sommelier may feel that your complaint is unjustified. But instead of arguing with you, he or she may tactfully suggest that you switch to another type of wine. This is a good opportunity to use a sommelier's expertise to explore new areas instead of insisting on the same wine, or same type of wine, every time: merely fulfilling your own expectations takes the excitement out of your dining experience and eventually makes you rather indifferent to the taste of that wine. In fact, you should take advantage of the sommelier's guidance to branch out and try something different right from the start, not just when a problem comes up.

White wine with meat of a rosy hue? Why not? Besides, if you really don't like the results of the sommelier's recommendation, he or she can hardly quibble if you insist on another wine, free of charge.

What if I have doubts about the wine when I taste it, but can't explain why?

It's not always easy to come out with a considered opinion of the wine while the sommelier or server is hovering over you, bottle in hand. Ideally, you should calmly concentrate on tasting. If you're intimidated by the circumstances, you can ask for a private moment with your wine, free from the pressure of the restaurant staff – after all, you are the one who is paying for the bottle.

Whether you're able to stake out your territory or not, don't hesitate to ask your dining companions what they think of the wine if you're still not sure; they may confirm your initial impression. You may find that the wine has a mild or strong corked taste, has some other bizarre odour or taste, or is vinegary. Express your first impression as precisely as you can and taste the wine again, individually or severally. Then, if there still seems to be a valid reason for doubt, advise the sommelier or server.

Don't be afraid: if the restaurant is a reputable establishment, no one is going to try to twist your arm or cheat you. Sending the bottle back won't cause an uproar or sabotage the meal. While the customer may no longer be an absolute monarch these days, he or she still wields enough power to exercise this prerogative – especially since the restaurant will be refunded by the supplier for a defective product.

What should I do when the cork is pointedly handed to me at a restaurant?

In the past, the cork was presented to show that it was in good condition (not fissured, crumbling, or mildewed) and for the diner to double-check the wine's origin by reading the name – and occasionally the vintage – branded on the cork.

Today, some wine experts sniff the "mirror" (the wine-soaked end) of the cork before tasting the liquid in the glass, affirming that it warns them beforehand if the wine is corked. They are right: a sick cork that has contaminated the wine with an unpleasant smell and taste will betray itself by the odour of cork taint. In other words, it doesn't only smell of wholesome, natural cork: it exudes a rank, often chemical odour.

A mere hint of off-smell in the cork, however, does not constitute a solid enough basis for rejecting the wine straight away. You must smell, and preferably also taste the wine to confirm your suspicions. It's really overdoing it, after barely sniffing the cork, to send it – and the wine with it – back to where it came from.

Yes, it is useful to smell the cork when it's placed in front of you, or handed to you when the bottle is opened at the table. But this should not be an obligatory inspection, nor a conclusive one. Better to smell and taste the wine in the glass, then, if any doubt remains, let it make a round of the table to obtain a consensus. After that, it's either bottoms up or back to the cellar for a replacement.

Is it rude to ask the restaurant staff to refrain from continually replenishing the wine glasses on the table?

Not at all. If you're a true wine enthusiast, don't hesitate to say that you would prefer to pour the wine yourself. You may not prevail at first, as many busy waiters and waitresses seem to perform this unwanted service automatically, no matter what they are told at the beginning of the meal.[1]

If you're too shy to repeat your request, or if you can see that it's pointless, you might ask them to stop pouring when the glass is one-third full, to derive the maximum benefit from the wine's aromas – even if your sniffing has to be done discreetly in this setting. You really should be allowed to drink the wine to the bottom before more is added: some aromas only emerge when there is a good amount of air inside the glass.

The restaurant staff may have instructions from the manager to rush over and fill up the glasses whenever possible. Obviously, the faster the

---

1. From the restaurant's point of view, if you serve yourself, it might lower the other diners' opinion of the service.

glasses are refilled, the sooner the bottle will be empty, making it likely that another one will be ordered – to the profit of the establishment.

If the waiter or waitress doesn't seem to hear your requests, remember that the wine, like the contents of your plate, belongs to you! Be brave and express your wishes more forcefully.

Is it worth trying the house wine in restaurants?

The quality of the *vin de la maison* or the *vin du patron* will be in keeping with the reputation of the particular restaurant.

Try to find out as much as you can about the house wine, or the wine sold by the glass. If there is a choice in this latter category, you could ask: "Which is the most popular of the wines that you sell by the glass?" The wine most in demand is more likely to have been freshly opened and thus be less affected by oxidation. You can also ask for specific details about the house wine – country and region of origin, if the vintage is specified, etc.

Restaurant house wines sold by the litre, half-litre, or quarter-litre are often the ten- or twenty-litre bag-in-box variety, and are not necessarily of poor quality. Try them when you want to save money, or if you consider that the type of food you have ordered calls for an ordinary wine.

Are there "all-purpose" wines that go well with a wide variety of dishes?

White wine, because of its lack of tannins, is more versatile and can be drunk with a wider variety of cuisines than red. To give an example, in Germany, the sweetish Auslese Riesling may be served with lamb. I can assure you, having tried it, that neither the wine nor the dish suffers.

Let's face it, though: if only from the point of view of colour harmony, a bottle of red looks much more appropriate on a table featuring a rack of lamb or a rare steak, lightly peppered and served with homemade french-fries.

Many people feel that New World wines, red as well as white, go well with almost any dish. According to them, these wines possess the body and fruitiness necessary to stand up to the most incongruous or exotic inspirations of today's haute cuisine, as well as any number of robust ethnic dishes.

What kind of wine should be served if one diner at the table orders fish, and another steak tartare?

In this particular example, either a Pinot Gris or a white Rhône wine can accommodate both the fish and the meat. Otherwise, when the choice of a single wine for disparate menu items seems more reckless than well advised, you can always order glasses or quarter-litres of the house red and white, or half-bottles (alas, rarely available in restaurants) of each type. A medium-bodied red (Burgundy or Chianti) will go well with the steak tartare if it's not too spicy, and a white wine can be chosen for the fish.

Also, keep in mind that rosé goes well with pasta and most white meat (veal, poultry, and pork).

The wine is already cool enough, but the waiter keeps putting it back into the ice bucket!

Don't think that this is done deliberately to annoy you: the staff is often so busy that it's probably just an unthinking, automatic gesture. But you must be on your toes and take the bottle out of the bucket whenever necessary, to let it thaw out on the table. Tell the confused waiter or waitress in passing that you want to keep the bucket in case the wine eventually needs further chilling.

■ Are crystals at the bottom of the bottle a fault?

The presence of crystals is certainly no reason to send the wine back, or even to call the sommelier.

When the temperature is low enough, tartaric acid, a natural ingredient of grapes, combines with the equally natural potassium in the bottle to create potassium bitartrate, a precipitate that solidifies into crystals and sinks to the bottom. The crystals, which resemble coarse salt crystals, may also stick to the bottom of the cork if the bottle has been stored on its side.

This natural phenomenon does not alter the wine. On the contrary, it indicates that the wine was not manipulated much before being bottled – a sign of good quality, in most cases. European wine growers justly take pride in the presence of crystals, referring to them as the "wine's diamonds." On the other side of the Atlantic, however, consumers are still suspicious when they find the whitish deposits in a bottle of wine: they imagine that the wine has undergone dubious processes or alterations such as the overzealous addition of sugar or stabilizing agents, or even that these inoffensive crystals are bits of broken glass!

If you swallow bitartrate crystals, absolutely nothing will happen to you. They are tasteless and odourless, although their texture may give the wine an abrasive feel in the mouth.[2]

---

2. Icewines, Sauternes, and other dessert wines often have a high concentration of tartaric acid. This is because the sweeter the wine, the more acidity it needs to stay fresh. Red wines, with their low acidity, do not usually allow these crystals to form, although they are not totally exempt from it. Another reason that reds are less susceptible is that they are rarely kept at the low temperatures (in the refrigerator, for example) that encourage the formation of bitartrate crystals.

Our meal at La Pergola was almost over when D., a wine connoisseur friend, stopped at our table, looked at our bottle, asked for a taste, then categorically declared that the wine we had been enjoying was corked!

D on't despair: even experienced tasters have trouble recognizing cork taint when a wine is only marginally affected by it. Presuming that your friend was not suffering from a case of sour grapes and making the whole thing up, you should have taken advantage of the circumstance to smell the wine more attentively, imprinting the odour in your memory for the future. The next time it happened, you'd be able to detect it more easily.

[Section 6]
Preserving Wine

French Proverb:

Treat wine kindly, and it will live long. But needless to say, it's pointless to pamper it if you mean it to tarry but one short day.

On a day-to-day basis, where should we keep a bottle of wine meant for the following evening or for the coming weekend?

Wine is above all sensitive to heat and light. It should at least be given the same consideration that you would give a dish of mayonnaise or butter, that is, you wouldn't leave it on top of the stove or on a sunny kitchen counter. Put the wine in a dark corner of the kitchen or in a cupboard – it doesn't matter much, especially if it's just for a day or two.

How long can a bottle of wine be kept around the house before drinking?

First of all, don't leave the wine in the refrigerator for months on end, although white wine – no one knows why – tolerates longer periods in the refrigerator than red does.

Out of the fridge, at room temperature and preferably in the shade or in the dark, most unopened wines will keep comparatively well for months, if not years.

Should wine bottles be stored on their sides, and if so, why?

I n principal, they should. When natural corks are used, laying the bottle horizontally brings the wine into contact with the cork, which keeps the cork's "mirror" moist and prevents it from drying out and shrinking. If the bottle is stored vertically for a long period, air may infiltrate between the cork and the inner surface of the bottle neck, and the wine will quickly oxidate and spoil.[1]

Normally, it takes several months for a cork to start shrinking when the bottle is standing upright, but in dry conditions, like those that exist inside our heated homes during the northern winter, the process is accelerated.

Thus, while bottles lying on their sides can be safely kept at room temperature for months without any danger, when a bottle has always been stored vertically, you shouldn't expect too much of the wine after the crucial turning point of six to eight months.

The exception to the rule are bottles with metal screw-on caps, which can be left standing. However, even wine sealed by a metal cap does not have an infinite life span, no matter how well it is protected from oxidation. It will still spoil eventually.

Do synthetic corks give better results? Some wine bottles with synthetic resin corks are sealed by a circular wax tab instead of the customary capsule (made of aluminium, plastic, or, in the case of fine vintage wines, tin). Wax, contrary to what homemade jam- and jelly-makers would have us believe, is not impermeable. It too "breathes"; a minute quantity of air passes through it.

As for the synthetic resin itself, it does not dry out, and therefore cannot shrink. Unfortunately, recent studies have shown that although the synthetic cork is waterproof and supposedly airtight,

---

1. This has not actually been scientifically demonstrated. It may well be that even when bottles are stored upright, natural corks keep them airtight. However, as long as doubt about this persists, it is better not to take a chance.

it, like any kind of plastic, can be permeated by gas – and therefore by air, making it potentially subject to oxidation. Besides that, we have already mentioned the faint hint of vinyl odour that some people's noses are able to detect in synthetically corked wine.

■ Isn't port stored vertically in cellars?

No, it isn't, and for the same reasons given above. Even the humbler brands of port, with their cork-and-plastic stoppers, are laid horizontally while they age in the bottle.

Since you've probably realized by now that there are no immutable truths in the world of wine, I'll tell you that opinions diverge on this subject too. Several reputable wine writers recommend that port and other fortified wines remain upright. The very trustworthy *Alexis Lichine's Encyclopedia of Wines and Spirits* specifies that this is not because the surplus alcohol in these wines may eventually corrode the cork, and adds that "it is precisely this high degree of alcohol that protects them from oxidation."

The Reading of the Will

"To my beloved son, who gave me such a marvellous sense of pride ever since the day he was born, I leave his deceased mother's silverware that he was always nagging me for. As for my dear daughter Sophie, who made my hair turn prematurely white, I would like to take advantage of this solemn occasion to say to her: give wine a chance. Answer the call of the vocation that I always felt was yours. Start your own collection; set up your own cellar, and have the whole authenticated by the notary here present. Do this and you will inherit my twelve magnums of 1995 Mouton-Rothschild... "

What is the advantage of having a personal wine cellar?

The great advantage of keeping your own cellar is to have on hand a reserve of ordinary and exceptional bottles of wine that you can open at the drop of a hat – if an unexpected occasion comes up, for example – saving you a trip to the wine store or liquor commission. It's like having a wine store at home! Besides ensuring that you're always well stocked, it's a buffer against the inevitable and frequent rises in wine prices.

Are those the only reasons for having a wine cellar?

Beyond these excellent practical reasons, when you start to really know and appreciate wine, it's a natural course of action. A wine enthusiast without a cellar is the equivalent of a music-lover who can only listen to music at concerts or at a friend's house.

Doesn't it cost a lot to set up a proper cellar?

A passion for wine can be a money-consuming habit. Great wines are expensive, and they tend to be bought by two categories of consumers, if I may put it in a caricatural way: by very wealthy people for whom the stock market holds no secrets, and by down-and-out students who pool the money from their student loans to indulge their elite taste in wine – with you and me paying the bill, in one way or another, for both categories.

There are rich people, and there are wine fanatics, and sometimes the two attributes combine in a few fortunate individuals. Kidding aside, you only have to frequent your local wine store or liquor commission to see that, these days, people from all levels of society are fascinated by wine.

This does not mean, unfortunately, that all wines are accessible to everyone. The days when a very good classified-growth Bordeaux could be had for $25 or $30 are long gone, and it seems that quality-price advantages are continually eroding. Nonetheless, the heart has its reasons...

How should I start setting up my cellar (even if it has to be on a buy-now, pay-later basis)?

Find the best place to store the bottles: in the basement, in a closet, or even at a friend or neighbour's house. Essentially, the location should be as cool and dark as possible. Once these two basic conditions are met, the questions of humidity and odours can be resolved.

That's why I gave up the first time: all those considerations of humidity, odours, vibrations, temperature, etc., made it seem too complicated.

It is complicated, and cellar experts haven't yet reached definite conclusions about some of these questions. However, there is a consensus regarding six basic requirements which I will deal with below, as simply as I can.

Temperature in the wine cellar: Everything will be fine if the temperature in the cellar does not go below 10-12°C (50-54°F) in winter or above 23-24°C (74-77°F) at the peak of the summer heat.

Heat is more to be feared than cold, as long as the wine doesn't freeze, which occurs at about -5°C (24°F). The temperature change should be gradual, like the change of seasons. An unacceptable fluctuation would be about 10°C (50°F) lower at night than in the daytime. However this kind of temperature variation is rare inside a residence.

Under the normal climatic conditions that prevail in most of North America – although these are far from ideal – wine will keep reasonably well. To illustrate, a wine laid down in a place where the temperature is a constant 12°C (54°F) starts to "die" (lose its fruit and vivacity) after about fifteen years, whereas the same wine, kept under the "normal" conditions described above, will begin to decline after ten or twelve years. It will age more quickly, but it will taste almost as good within its preservation limit.

Humidity in the wine cellar: It should never be under 50%. Over that median, the relative humidity can be as high as 95% and even 100% without doing any harm, except to labels, which may become spotted with mildew. It is not difficult to maintain sufficient humidity during the summer in most of North America, whereas in winter, our homes become very dry, and it may be necessary to install a humidifier in the wine cellar, just as we do in the main part of the house or apartment. The humidifier should be equipped with a hygrostat which keeps the humidity at a constant level.

Why is so much humidity necessary? To prevent corks from drying out, say almost all of the world's wine experts. But, as we have seen, simply tilting the bottles at the proper angle keeps their corks moist, preventing shrinkage and air infiltration. The great importance of humidity lies in the demonstrable (although unexplained) fact that it – at 70% and above – significantly slows down the aging process, as do cooler temperatures.[2]

---

2. More than once, I have tasted a great wine that had been kept in a cool (12°C; 54°F) but insufficiently humid cellar (only 40%). It was clear that it had evolved more quickly under these conditions than bottles of the same wine stored at the same temperature in a more humid atmosphere (60-70%).

Odours in the wine cellar: If there are no predominant odours in your wine cellar at the start, no problems should ensue. Just remember that wine demands exclusivity: no vegetables, preserves, paint cans, or detergents should be anywhere near it. If the wine is to be kept inside a closet or cupboard, put your head inside and sniff the air at the back. If you don't detect any odour, it means that all is well.

Ventilation of the wine cellar: There is no need for a vent or any other air-circulation system in the wine cellar. The opening and closing of the door when you visit the cellar should be enough to renew the air inside. Even if you leave for a few weeks' vacation, don't worry: it would take longer than that for the cellar to develop a stuffy, closed-in odour.

Vibrations in the wine cellar: Chemists who have studied how vibrations affect wine are unanimous in stating that alterations occur only on a molecular level and that the vibrations must be at a very high frequency to do any damage. Therefore, you shouldn't worry about the thumping spin-cycle of the washing machine, or your adolescent's stomping footsteps and pounding rock music. The worst that can happen when a bottle is agitated – even if you take it in your hand and shake it vigorously – is that the sediment will be suspended throughout the wine for a while. But that's all. No dramatic inner transformation will have occurred.

Lighting in the wine cellar: As you do when you go into the pantry or a large closet, you switch the light on when you enter your cellar and turn it off when you leave. If you forget to turn off the light and it stays on for a whole day or night, the wine will not be affected by so little. But remember to keep it in the dark in the long term.

Most houses and other types of residential buildings have a level that is at least partially underground, making it easy to meet the necessary requirements of darkness, coolness, and humidity.

What about portable wine cellars, especially if there is no basement? Aren't they regulated so that you don't have to bother with all these details?

True: apartment wine cellars are basically refrigerators in which not only the temperature, but the humidity and the vibrations are automatically controlled. The cabinet-style cellars with wooden or glass doors may be quite elaborately finished. There are even walk-in portable cellars. Prices vary a lot, according to size (defined according to bottle capacity – 100-bottle, 200- or 300-bottle, etc.), function features, parts and materials used, as well as the quality of workmanship of the cellar, which is, after all, a piece of furniture.

The cabinet cellar is definitely the dream solution for wine collectors – on paper at least. Since the microenvironment is rigorously controlled, elements of chance are eliminated. You don't have to worry or even think about your wine storage unit: just open it and select a bottle.

In reality, besides the fact that these refrigerator-cabinets are expensive (about $2000 for the 200-bottle model) and in spite of improvements made in recent years, the portable wine cellars available in North America may still be subject to mechanical glitches. The compressor might stop working in the middle of a heat wave, for example. Although the manufacturers and distributors usually provide good guarantees, that's not much of a comfort to you if your favourite wines have heated up to 30°C (86°F) and will stay at that temperature until the cellar is repaired.

All things considered, are portable cellars reliable?

If you are looking for the ideal wine conservation system, and if you tend to be a worrywart and a perfectionist, it's probably worth your while to buy the latest portable cellar. It would be even better to buy a specialized air conditioner for your basement wine cellar or cupboard. You can keep it running from June to October, more or less, and the cellar can be left undisturbed. Unlike ordinary air conditioners, it doesn't dry out the atmosphere, nor does it need an evacuation vent to get rid of the condensation and the warm air. Moreover, no ordinary air conditioner can continually maintain the temperature below 15°C (59°F).

▌I'm quite good at home repairs. Couldn't I build a cellar myself?

Yes, if you don't insist on state-of-the-art specifications and are willing to give and take a little in the building process. There's even a good do-it-yourself book to help you: *How and Why to Build a Wine Cellar.*[3]

If you're handy at carpentry, you probably won't need any instructions for shelves and counters. Remember that it's important that the structure be firm and solid, and that the shelves allow the bottles to slant in such a way that, while the cork stays in contact with the wine, the sediment will sink to the bottom.

In other words, the air inside should be situated in the "shoulder" of a Bordeaux-type bottle. Also, slightly tilting the bottles bottom-downwards instead of strictly horizontally prevents them from slipping out and causing loss as well as a mess.

A word of warning if you decide to create your original cellar: don't use pressboard or plywood, as the smell of the glue in them can affect the wine.

---

3. This classic, published in 1983 with later re-editions, is available through the Internet or from the author: Richard M. Gold, Sandhill Publishing, P.O. Box 9614, North Amherst, MA 01059, U.S.A.; Tel. (413) 549-0841; golddesch@aol.com. You might find a copy at your local library.

I'm useless at woodwork. Can I still set up my own cellar?

Y ou do have a few options, available in wine accessory stores. Note, however, that terracotta pipes, although they look charmingly rustic and help stabilize the temperature, take up a lot of unnecessary room. A wine collection tends to expand sooner than you expect, and this choice of wine holder will not leave you much leeway.

Also, avoid using the wines' original cardboard cases: with the high humidity that a good cellar requires, the boxes will soften and fall apart. Conversely, if the cellar is dry, the cardboard will suck up precious humidity.

Condo Owners' Meeting

"Welcome everyone to the August general meeting! The priority items on the agenda are the landscaping, the wall between our building and the building to the north of us, and our treasurer's proposal to strengthen our community spirit by investing in a collective wine cellar.

"On this last subject, although it's already been established where the cellar will be situated, there are a number of details that have to be ironed out. I confess, I find all the ramifications a bit overwhelming, but our resident oenophile and treasurer has assured me, and she'll explain it to all of you later, that she'll be available to oversee the project... right down to the last drop, as she says."

All right! I'm ready to start keeping wine in a cellar. What should I buy first?

Not so fast: before you start, you should estimate how much of your monthly budget can be dedicated to this pastime. Be realistic without being too reticent: after all, a passion implies a measure of excess, with some inevitable sacrifices. If you overspend $150 at the wine store or liquor commission one afternoon, don't reduce your wine expenses during the weeks following. Instead, I suggest (at the risk of sounding callous) that you cut down on clothes, restaurants, the children's outings, or any other non-essential!

Once you've started your cellar, the key to success (Rule No. 1) is constancy and regularity. There wouldn't be much sense in buying twenty bottles at once and drinking them one after the other, without adding to the cellar until you've finished them all.

Give yourself a quantity objective: let's say thirty bottles at the beginning to make the cellar look inhabited, then six bottles every month. At this rate, presuming you're strong-willed enough not to dip into your growing reserve too often (this is Rule No. 2, by the way), you'll have an impressive collection of over a hundred bottles before a year has gone by.

When this critical mass is attained, you'll have to decide if a supply of this size suits your purposes, or if, for all sorts of reasons, you should go beyond it. If you decide that the hundred or so bottles in your cellar are enough for your purposes, then, your only further duty will be to replace each bottle that you take from the cellar to drink (Rule No. 3).

If the passion for wine has taken root deep inside you – if it has touched your soul and irrevocably transformed your attitude to life, as it tends to do – you'll undoubtedly find the necessary means to multiply the number of bottles in your cellar exponentially, up to one, two, or even three thousand bottles, clearly an excessive number for one household!

Is there one type of wine that should constitute the basis of my cellar? Or should I diversify from the start?

First, you should differentiate between wines to be laid down for future drinking, and those to be drunk now – the current reserve. This will save you from having to go to the store all the time.

Thus, parallel to the wines chosen for aging, you can place about a dozen bottles for everyday consumption on a more accessible shelf. This "emergency stock" should consist of reds, whites, and a couple of dessert wines, all within the $12-$15 range. Replenish this section periodically with equivalent wines, in the same way that you replace your long-term wines.

As with any other purchase, we buy the wines that we like. These might include some favourite Bordeaux, Burgundy, Chianti, Niagara, or California wines. But try to introduce a little more variety so that you'll be prepared for special occasions and also be able to come up with the appropriate wine for any kind of meal.

As for deciding exactly which wines should be purchased, we don't have that many alternatives: we can keep up with the suggestions in wine columns in newspapers and magazines, and with the recommendations in the wine guides that are published annually. Good books on wine are also appearing in greater numbers every year. We can also check the Internet for further discoveries, and, last but not least, we can consult some of the dedicated wine advisers who work in wine stores, many of whom adore their jobs.[4]

---

4. How can you tell if wine counsellors are really passionate about wine? Ask them a question or two and observe the way they answer. If they obviously take the trouble to answer to the best of their knowledge, if they become excited, and above all, if they give more information than you have actually sought (for example: "I'm sorry, we're out of it. But have you tried the latest Graillot Crozes-Hermitages by any chance? Absolutely marvellous!") then, you'll know you've found a great source. Seek out this person for all your new wine purchases and you'll be well served.

Regardless of the particular wine chosen for its aging potential, a good strategy is to buy a minimum of three bottles of it. Open the first bottle soon after purchase – even if you have the painful impression that you are depleting your life's blood. Drink the second bottle one year later, and keep the third one for about four or five years before drinking. Then, even if you don't always make tasting notes on all your bottles, you'll still be able to follow the evolution of that wine and appreciate its improvement over a patiently endured – but not too long! – maturation period.

Include a good number of half-bottles in your collection – of port and other fortified wines, as well as dry whites and reds. This is a very convenient format, although wine ages faster in the half-bottle than in the standard 750-ml (16-oz.) format. Some suggestions for half-bottles that are usually available in the provincial liquor commissions are: Pfaffenheim Tokay-Pinot Gris and Hugel Riesling (both from Alsace); red and white Mouton-Cadet (Bordeaux); Chablis Bichot (Burgundy); also suggested are quarter-bottles of red and white Cellier des Dauphins (Rhône); Fortant de France Merlot or Cabernet (Languedoc); Chianti Ruffino (Tuscany).

Isn't really good wine supposed to keep for decades?

Wines that still improve after twenty years in the bottle are extremely rare, and those that are not quite ready to drink after ten years are almost as rare. The majority, close to the totality of wines, in fact, are practically at their apogee as soon as they reach the shelves of liquor stores, or, at the most, within five years after the harvest year indicated on the label.

■ What is a cellar log?

I t's a register of the cellar's contents. Don't bother buying the expensive versions sold in wine accessory stores – most are just bound photocopies – that will supposedly make your life easier. You can produce your own log simply by opening a computer file. Every time you buy a wine, register it in the log: number of bottles purchased, name, vintage, place and date of purchase, and price. For example (in the Rhône section):

4 Château de Beaucastel 1999
York St. store, Sept. 2003, $59

The cellar log is a detailed inventory of your wine heritage, to which you can periodically add comments. The wine cellar itself is an evolving organism that you are continually subtracting from and adding to. Thus, when you drink one of the bottles of the Châteauneuf-du-Pape listed in the above example a month after purchasing them, you would substitute the number 4 by the number 3, noting:

Drunk October 9 with Tamsin and Jiri. Closed – odourless and practically tasteless – but promising, considering density and concentration. Keep other bottles at least a year before trying again. Should be terrific with grilled lamb.

Make a couple of printouts of the log every few months to have an up-to-date copy on hand, and you'll have a good overall idea of your cellar's current assets.

[Off the Beaten Track]

H ere are some suggestions for a cellar in which most of the wine is intended for medium-term aging. Quite a few of the wines are not obvious choices, by which I hope that you will build up an original and interesting wine collection. The reds listed here can be laid down for five to seven years after the harvest date on the label. The whites (like the reds, to be replaced as soon as they go missing!) should be drunk between two and four years of age.

Rather than an exhaustive cellar guide, these suggestions are meant to indicate worthwhile directions that you can explore (in both reds and whites), off the beaten Bordeaux/Burgundy/Chianti track – as long as this appeals to you. You can also use the list of reliable wine producers that I have provided (on pages 139 and 140) to supplement your selections.

FRANCE

BEAUJOLAIS Reds of the Moulin-à-Vent appellation: the very good vintages (1990, 1996, 1999) sometimes keep well for ten or more years in the cellar (Château des Jacques, Domaine de Champ de Cour, Château du Moulin à Vent, Gay-Coperet, etc.).

RHÔNE VALLEY Northern Rhône reds of the Crozes-Hermitage appellation (Belle Père et Fils, Gilles Robin, Jaboulet Thalabert, Chapoutier Les Varonniers, Domaine des Rémizières, etc.); southern Rhône reds of the Gigondas appellation (Les Goubert, Clos des

Cazaux, Guigal, etc.) and reds of the Vacqueyras appellation (La Garrigue, Jaboulet, Clos des Cazaux, etc.).

SOUTHWEST Whites of the Jurançon appellation, sweet or dry (Cauhapé, Clos Uroulat, Étienne Brana) and Pacherenc du Vic-Bilh sweet whites (Château d'Aydie, Montus-Bouscassé, Cave de Crouseilles); reds of the Madiran appellation (Brumont, d'Aydie, Viella, etc.).

LANGUEDOC-ROUSSILLON Costières-de-Nîmes reds (Mourgues du Grès, Saint-Cyrgues, Château de Nages, Domaine du Mas Neuf, Mas des Bressades); Côtes-du-Roussillon reds (Domaine Cazes, Dona Baissas, La Cazenove, Sarda-Malet).

PROVENCE Bandol reds and whites (Pibarnon, Vannières, Pradeaux, etc.); reds of the Côtes-de-Provence and Les-Baux-de-Provence appellations (Château Réal Martin, Domaine Gavoty, Mas de Cadenet, Maîtres-Vignerons de la Presqu'île de Saint-Tropez, Sainte-Roseline, Château Romanin).

LOIRE Whites: dry or sweet Vouvray (Domaine Huet, Domaine des Aubusières); reds: Saumur-Champigny (Targé, Roches Neuves, Domaine Fouet, Château des Varrains, Château de Villeneuve), Chinon (Joguet, Couly-Dutheil, Bernard Baudry), Saint-Nicolas-de-Bourgueil (Yannick Amirault, Joël Taluau, Domaine des Ouches), and Touraine (Domaine Michaud, Domaine Sauvète).

ITALY

PIEDMONT Reds of the Barbera d'Asti *denominazione* (Chiarlo, Bava, Prunotto, Giacomo Bologna) and of the Dolcetto d'Alba DOC (Batasiolo, Pio Cesare, Renato Ratti).

VENETO The concentrated Amarone della Valpolicella reds (Tedeschi, Bolla, Masi, Tommasi, etc.).

TUSCANY Reds of the Rosso di Montalcino *denominazione* (Argiano, Caparzo, Castello Banfi, etc.).

THE MARCHES Whites of the Castelli di Jesi (Verdicchio) DOC (Umani-Ronchi, Garofoli, Fazi-Battaglia).

BASILICATA Reds of the Aglianico del Vuture appellation (Paternoster, D'Angelo).

APULIA Reds made from the Negro Amaro grape (Taurino, Casa Girelli, Leone de Castris, Candido).

SICILY Reds (Regaleali, Duca di Salaparuta).

SARDINIA Cannonau di Sardegna reds (Sella & Mosca, Argiolas, Santadi).

OTHER WINE REGIONS

GERMANY "Qualitätswein mit Prädikat" whites from all regions, of the Kabinett, Spätlese, and, if you can afford it, the Auslese types (producers: Dr. Loosen, Kesselstat, Juliusspital, Staatsweingüter, Egon Müller, Schloss Johannisberg, Toni Jost, etc.). These are agreeably sweet wines with a welcome crispness that are surprisingly long-lived, more so than many reds, in fact. They last up to ten years, easily.

CHILE The super-Chileans (red), if their prices don't scare you off (Seña, Clos Apalta, Montes "M," etc.); the much more affordable Cabernet Sauvignon Antigas Riservas, made by Cousiño-Macul, and the flavourful Merlots made by Casa Lapostolle, among others.

SOUTH AFRICA Pinotage-based reds (Kanonkop, Zonnebloem, Simonsig, etc.) and Cabernet Sauvignon-based reds (Le Bonheur, Rust-en-Vrede, Plaisir de Merle, Backsberg, Meerlust, etc.).

AUSTRALIA Cabernet/Shiraz blends (Rosemount Estates, Penfolds, D'Arenberg, De Bortoli, Coldstream Hills, Brown Brothers, Château Tahbilk, Penley Estate, Yalumba, etc.).

PORTUGAL Dry reds of the Douro, Palmela, and Dão appellations (Luís Pato, Esporão, Sogrape, Aliança, etc.); red Periquita made by José Maria da Fonseca.

SPAIN Almost any wines produced by Miguel Torres in the Penedès region of Catalonia (Gran Sangre de Toro, Mas la Plana, etc.); the fine Ribera del Duero reds, Alion, Prado Rey, Pesquera, and Hacienda Monasterio; from Rioja, Marqués de Cáceres, Conde de Valdemar (Martinez Bujanda) and Viña Ijalba; Carchelo (Agapito Rico) from the Jumilla region south of Valencia.

DESSERT WINES

FRANCE Rivesaltes, Maury, and Banyuls wines of the Roussillon (Casa Blanca, Docteur Parcé, Cazes Frères, Mas Amiel, Puig-Parahy, La Tour Vieille, Gilles Baissas); aged red and white Pineau-des-Charentes (Montifaud, Château de Beaulon); Loire Valley (Jo Pithon, Philippe Delesvaux, Patrick Baudoin); Gaillac in the Southwest region (Domaine de Causses Marines, Robert Plageoles, etc.).

SPAIN Amontillado or oloroso sherry (Lustau, Hidalgo, Domecq, Williams & Humbert, etc.).

ITALY Vin Santo (Lungarotti, Ricasoli, Isole e Olena, Frescobaldi, Antinori) and Moscato Passito di Pantelleria (Donnafugata, Pellegrino).

AUSTRALIA The incredibly sweet, fruity muscats of Buller, Morris, etc.

SOUTH AFRICA Vin de Constance and Noble Late Harvest (Klein Constantia, Nederburg, Delaire, Cathedral Cellar, Van Loveren, etc.).

HUNGARY Tokay Aszú, 4 Puttonyos or more (Disznoko, Oremus, Pajzos, Royal Tokaji).

PORTUGAL Setúbal Moscatel (José Maria da Fonseca, Horacio Simões).

CANADA Late harvest whites (Cave Spring, Vineland Estates, Quails' Gate, Konzelmann) and the vast majority of Riesling-based icewines – all delicious but, alas, all much too expensive.

UNITED STATES Vin de Glacière Muscat (Boony Doon) and Johannisberg Riesling (Château St. Jean/Beringer).

CHILE Late harvest Sauvignon Blancs (Errazuriz, House of Morandé).

Between Heaven and Earth

Question: I was born in Burgundy, at Nuits-Saint-Georges, between the 20th and 30th of September, most likely between 8 a.m. and 3 p.m. I would like to know what the future holds for my owner as far as my freshness and longevity is concerned, as well as on the financial level – will I prove to be a good investment? Also, will I travel? Will I be exchanged?

The Astrologer's Reply: Your sun sign is Libra and your ascendant is Aquarius, indicating that you have a contradictory character. One side of you is frank and friendly, while the other is secretive and sly. You will soon enter a period of stealthy concealment during which you will be closed and inexpressive. Your owner will be horrified by your taciturnity and will seriously consider trading you in for a more affable and open companion. Your relationship will be turbulent, to say the least.

But the future is not all dark. Before long, you will bounce back, bursting with freshness after your exile in the desert. Like the prodigal son, you will spread joy and delectation around you.

As for travelling, why not? It won't be the last time that a first growth like you moves to another cellar, only to find that a change is not always for the better!

Jupiter's influence will prevail just before you turn twenty, and the time for your retirement – some might say early retirement – will arrive. With the moon in your ninth house, your owner would still be able to pass you off as "a great Nuits in its plateau of maturity," and sell you, although you and I would know, if this occurs, that your years of glory are behind you. Any new owner would inevitably discover that your life force is spent, and would treat you with cold indifference.

However, with a lenient Scorpion and harmonizing opposites in Venus, I can see that you have an amazing lucky streak, and can probably avoid all this stress. What are you waiting for to convert to biodynamic principles?

How can you tell before opening a bottle of wine if it's ready for drinking?

There is no sure-fire way of knowing. Two bottles of the same vintage, from the same shipment, even from the same case, may be drunk at the same stage of their evolution and still taste quite different.

Trying to pinpoint a wine's peak, or more approximately, to estimate its plateau of maturity, is tricky. While one person may consider it ready for drinking at a certain point, another may find that it is drying out and in decline. Sometimes individual perspectives reflect national tastes. For example, the British (in general) think that a good Bordeaux shouldn't be opened until it has aged from fifteen to twenty years. Many French and North American wine lovers, on the other hand, prefer fruity young wines to the mushroom, plum, and leafy aromas of venerable aged wines.

There are a few ways to verify if a bottle of wine is past its prime. You can examine its colour by holding the bottle against a light source and looking through the lower part of the neck. If you notice a distinctly orange hue in a red wine, it is probably at its peak. In green-tinted bottles of white wine, it's almost impossible to gauge the wine's freshness by its colour, whereas in clear bottles, changes in the colour of white wine are more apparent, particularly in the case of Sauternes. Its various degrees of golden-yellow (when young) darken progressively to glowing amber, and after three or four decades, to bronze.

Accumulated sediment is not an indicator of decline unless you know that there was no sediment to begin with (when the wine was brought to market), or that it wasn't stored at a low temperature (0-5°C or 24-32°F) for too long. In the latter case, the cold may have caused the formation of solid precipitates.

However, these visual examinations remain rather haphazard and vague. The surest way to know when a wine is ready for drinking (or at its peak) is to follow its evolution in your cellar by periodically tasting bottles from the same batch. You'll learn to judge whether more time is needed for the flavours to achieve a better balance or for the acidity to attenuate, or, conversely, whether you should drink the other bottles of that particular wine over the next few months, before it loses its charm.

Are vintage ratings a good guide to a wine's evolution?

Not really. The same goes for charts that indicate aging potential. These are very general. They don't usually take into account the remarkable differences that may exist between wines from the same region. Take the Rhône Valley, for example. In a particular year, good weather in the Northern Rhône may produce a great vintage, while torrential rain during the harvest period in the south puts the production at risk: the picking will be more difficult; rainwater will dilute the must and therefore the wine; and, finally, if the grapes receive little precious sunshine, they may not ripen sufficiently and – in the case of red wine – their skins will impart "green," less supple tannins.

Also, depending on the appellation – and above all on the particular grower – some wines are superior, year after year, to those of other producers whose vineyards are in the same region and are subject to the same climatic conditions.[5] The crucial difference may lie in better soil drainage.

Wine writers, tasters, and connoisseurs in general readily acknowledge the inherent grey areas in vintage ratings, which remain, at best, a supplementary element to help us make a final choice when we buy wine.

Taking all this into account, as well as the fact that over the last twenty years, the quasi-totality of the vintages in the principal wine-growing regions of the world were qualified as "honest" at worst and more often as "very good," it is clear that vintage-rating charts are not essential. Perhaps they are not even useful as an accessory, but are in fact practically superfluous to an otherwise well-informed choice.

Luckily, with today's knowledge and technology, off-years in which we don't see the production of even a single good wine have practically ceased to exist.

---

5. Very warm years, with an ideal amount of sun and rain at the right times, provide excellent raw material, but wine growers must know how to contain this bounty. However, if the resulting wine is over-extracted in the process, it loses in elegance what it gains in concentration and fullness.

[Evolution of the Principal Types of Wine]

T he table on the following two pages gives the approximate lengths of time that different wines will stay fresh and good to drink, assuming they are stored, right after purchase, in a passive, temperature-controlled atmosphere – that is, at a temperature which rises and falls gradually and does not exceed lows of 8-10°C (47-50°F) in winter and highs of 22-24°C (72-76°F) in summer.[6] The humidity rate should be 50% or above.

It is also assumed that the wines listed come from reputable wineries, were made during good (though not necessarily exceptional) vintage years, and that the people who will drink them are more interested in the fruity aromas and flavours of young wine, even if this implies a high dose of tannins or acidity, which will, to a certain extent, be toned down by any accompanying food.

---

6. The weak link in the chain of wine preservation is the delivery from the winery to the point of sale. Wine travels by ship, and containers are rarely air-conditioned. Unless the wine is kept in the hold, that is, under the waterline, it runs an obvious risk of overheating, especially if it is kept on deck in the middle of summer, or on the dock before and after sailing – one more reason that you should sample one bottle in a batch as soon as you buy it. The refund deadline is usually one year at most provincial government liquor outlets in Canada; American wine stores may be reluctant to refund wine more than a few months after purchase.

[From the harvest date indicated on the label]

	Age of fruitiness and freshness	Age of maturity and suppleness	Age of decline: time to go your separate ways
DRY WHITE WINES In general:	1-2 years	2-4 years	over 4 years
Exceptions: the best white Burgundy and Bordeaux	3-7 years	7-9 years	over 10 years
Vouvray, Savennières, Hermitage	5-8 years	8-15 years	over 15 years
ROSÉS AND VINS NOUVEAUX	Rosés should be drunk within 1 year after the harvest; *vins nouveaux* as soon as they reach the store in November, in any case, before Christmas		
CHAMPAGNE from the date of purchase	1-3 years		over 3 years
Exception: vintage Champagne, from the harvest year indicated on the label	5-8 years	8-12 years	over 12 years
LIGHT-BODIED RED WINES Beaujolais, ordinary Burgundy, Anjou, Touraine, etc. In general:	1-2 years	3-4 years	over 4 years
Exceptions: Fine Burgundy, the best Beaujolais – Morgon and Moulin-à-Vent appellations	2-5 years	5-8 years	over 8 years
MEDIUM-BODIED RED WINES ordinary Bordeaux, Chianti, Rioja, New World Pinot Noir and Merlot, Languedoc, etc. In general:	2-4 years	4-5 years	over 5 years
Exceptions: Classified-growth Bordeaux	3-8 years	8-15 years	over 15 years

	Age of fruitiness and freshness	Age of maturity and suppleness	Age of decline: time to go your separate ways
FULL-BODIED RED WINES Châteauneuf-du-Pape, Gigondas, Cairanne, Roussillon, Douro, Madiran, Zinfandel, Pinotage, etc.)			
In general:	2-5 years	5-7 years	over 7 years
Exceptions: Fine California Cabernet, Australian Shiraz, Italian Amarone, Barolo and Barbaresco	2-8 years	8-10 years	over 10 years
DESSERT AND FORTIFIED WHITE WINES In general: Sauternes, Alsatian *grains nobles*, etc.	2-6 years	6-12 years	over 12 years
Exceptions: Muscat and most New World dessert wines including icewines	2-3 years	3-4 years	over 4 years
Loire: Vouvray, Coteaux-du-Layon, Bonnezeaux, etc.	2-8 years	8-20 years	over 20 years
PORT LBV type	4-6 years	6-10 years	over 10 years
vintage port	3-10 years	10-20 years	over 20 years
tawny/colheita	Ready to drink when purchased; but will keep (without further aging), for several years.		
MISCELLANEOUS Rivesaltes, Maury, Vin Santo, Vin de Constance, Passito, etc.	2-6 years	6-10 years	over 10 years

N.B.: All of the above estimates are on the conservative side. It is always safer to drink a wine when it is too young than when it is too old. This applies to wines of all categories, except top classified growths produced in great vintage years, which tend to last considerably longer.

What does a wine that is stale and past its prime actually taste like?

Every wine, once its day is done, pretty much reverts to its primary state, that is, a mixture of water, alcohol, and acidity – as if its soul had departed, leaving its material remains behind. In old, practically decrepit wine, the high principal that gave the wine its spirit and eloquence, its animated, changing personality and its quotient of mystery, has gone forever.

White wine: Long before the wine's decline becomes evident to the eye (the colour gradually deepening to brown), it loses its crispness, its bracing and refreshing acidity. Its fruit aromas – apricot, lemon, peach, grapefruit, pear, etc. – completely vanish. It does not have a repulsive odour: it just smells wrong – of rancid nuts, camphor, or resin – revealing that oxidation has done its work.

Red wine: While the colour of red wine pales with age until it becomes brownish-orange (thus, old whites and old reds end up having practically the same tint), on the aroma front, the fruit of a red wine in decline either disappears or has a cooked flavour, often of stewed plums, with dusty earth notes. In the mouth, the tannins will have precipitated and sunk to the bottom of the bottle, taking with them the anthocyanin pigments, the basis of the colour extracted from the grape skins. In the end, the wine will dry out and its balance will be lost as acidity comes to predominate.[7]

The above descriptions summarize what eventually happens to all types of wine, dry or sweet, sparkling or still.

Another sure sign that a wine is on its way out is the loss of complexity – when you can only detect one aroma (no matter which one it may be) and can hardly taste anything at all. When a wine is young, its one-dimensional character may be a promise of better

---

7. The acidity as such does not increase: it is just more noticeable because of the tannins' defection. This is what causes the impression of angularity in red wines that are past their prime.

things to come, but if it has passed the preservation limit shown in the table on the pages 126 and 127, it is most likely beyond redemption.

> **I recently opened a bottle of wine from a case that I bought last year. It was a huge disappointment: the wine was mute and closed, even though it wasn't so young anymore. Strangely enough, the last bottle I tried four months ago was quite good. Does this mean that all the others in the case have started to decline? How could this have happened so quickly?**

The whole batch may indeed have gone into a sudden decline, but don't bet on it. If the wine has been kept in proper storage conditions and if it cannot be considered old, it may just be going through a mute, or dumb phase, during which it withdraws and becomes inarticulate.

If a wine has closed up in the bottle and you open it during this phase – which may last a few months, a year, or even two years – it will certainly be a letdown. The wine will seem very bland, and you'll regret having bought so many bottles of it; you may even curse the wine critic whose advice you followed so unquestioningly.

Great red Bordeaux, especially Médoc, occasionally suffers from stage fright between the fifth and seventh year after harvest (that is, between two and four years after bottling). Thus, at the beginning of 2004, for example, some of the red Bordeaux of the 1996 vintage will be just ending its mute phase. It will emerge transformed, its aromas modified and well-defined, its tannins more supple and caressing. The 1998 vintage may follow the same pattern. As for other great wines, both red and white, in principle, they are all potentially subject to this temporary imbalance.

Don't pull your hair out; in any case; you can't do anything about it – the wine has been bought and paid for, and the refund date has probably gone by. Surprises of this kind are not rare, but there is room for hope. Open another bottle in six months, and another, if you still have faith in the wine's intrinsic nobility and grandeur, two years later. You might be well rewarded for your patience.[8]

Letter to an Insurance Broker

Cherished friend,

I hope you're well. I'm afraid I can't say the same for us. Don't think I'm reporting our teenager's latest car crash! No, thank goodness, things seem to have calmed down in that department. I'm writing for a totally different reason.

Our basement was broken into when we were away last week! The only section that was padlocked was the wine cellar, and, you guessed it, the thief couldn't resist forcing the lock. You can imagine our horror on returning home: goodbye to our Volnays, our Chambertins, and I don't know what else! I haven't been able to estimate our total losses yet; my mind is still reeling.

---

8. The most spectacular instance of this kind that I had the pleasure of experiencing happened a few years ago, when a group of us wine lovers were terribly disappointed by our first taste of the 1983 Château Cos d'Estournel, a great Bordeaux of the Saint-Estèphe appellation. The wine's colour was dull, it had no perceptible aroma, was thin-bodied, and in a word, was dead awaiting burial. Twenty minutes later, we gave it another chance, tasting the wine we had left in our glasses. Revelation! The Cos had undergone an amazing transformation: its fruit emerged on the nose and its marvellous texture was clearly evident. Even its colour had deepened! A miracle? A hoax? Not so: the owner of the winery at that time, Bruno Prats, heard about the incident and wrote to us afterwards, explaining that, given a chance to breathe, the wine had absorbed the necessary oxygen to resuscitate.

You knew, I believe, that we were sitting on a veritable gold mine of Burgundy *grands crus*. I'm sure I remember, last summer at the golf club, asking you to include them in our policy...

■ Should the wine cellar be insured?

N
o. That is, it doesn't necessarily have to be insured separately from your regular policy. Wine is considered an item of personal property like any other, according to the Insurance Bureau of Canada (IBC). Just as you're covered by your home insurance policy for dropping your TV set from the top of the stairs, you're also covered for the damage when the bottom falls out of a wine case and the bottles smash all over your kitchen tiles – as long as you promptly bring the matter to the attention of your friendly insurance broker.

You'll also be covered for the loss of your precious wine if the house burns down or is flooded, or if the heating system breaks down in winter while you're away on holiday. You can claim up to the total value stipulated in your policy. The sticky point, as you might have guessed, is the rapid rise in value of a wine collection: a mere hundred bottles can easily represent several thousand dollars in potential claims.

If your wine collection is very valuable, yes, you can have it insured separately in a specific clause of your policy. It's worth having all-risk coverage for it, leaving no doubt that you will be compensated if the cellar's cooling system breaks down, for instance.

The fly in the ointment is that, in the words of the IBC: "Certain exclusions or restrictions may apply more particularly to this type of personal property, especially with regard to its storage and preservation." Thus, coverage can be limited on an article depending on the normal wear that it is likely to undergo, or if it is designated as fragile or breakable. Furthermore, "antiques, original art works, and similar objects... by their very nature, cannot be replaced by an equivalent new item," and compensation is limited to the value of the item at the time when the damage occurs.

The good news is that the amount awarded in compensation is nearly always higher than the purchase price, as even the insurers admit that fine wine rises in value as it ages. Thus, in spite of the impossibility of obtaining an equivalent, you'll still obtain fair restitution for your loss in terms of market value.

In the case of a dispute with the insurer – about whether or not the wine in your basement was affected when the sewer backed up, for example – the insurance company or broker must come to an agreement with you on the choice of an expert who will be called upon to settle the question. In Canada, when such cases arise, the experts consulted are often employees of the provincial government monopolies where the wine was bought.

Wine is made to drink, of course, but it's also an attractive investment proposal, given its rise in value over time. What do you think about speculating in wine?

First, face the facts. Even if you do manage to sell a couple of bottles at a profit once in a while, when you put it against the amount that you spend on wine altogether, you'll always be in the red.

If you're planning to collect wine solely on a speculative basis, it is possible to make a profit. But only the more spectacular *grands crus* that are always in demand will bring you an eventual benefit.

The difficulty will be to find buyers who will accept your word that the wine has been kept under optimum conditions.

[Section 7]
Understanding Wine

[Exploring the Jungle

Confusion sets in as soon as you enter one of the gigantic new liquor stores or wine emporiums. Just a glance at the first shelf is enough to boggle the mind: bottles of Cabernet Sauvignon here, bottles of Cabernet there, eight types of Chardonnay on the left, and an equal number of Merlots further over. How are you going to find your way through it all?

"I guarantee you," insists the store's wine consultant, "each one is different. Take these Chardonnays here. This one is more mineral, whereas the one at the end of the row has a heavy tropical-fruit nose. But if you're looking for something to go with Malpèque oysters, don't make the mistake of buying a New World Chardonnay. You need minerality and ripe, not jammy, fruit..."

How can there be so much diversity among wines made from the same grapes?

Just as it does in vegetable gardens, the soil plays an essential role in wine growing. Broadly speaking, it is the combination of soil and climate (the basis of what is termed the terroir) of a vineyard that gives us the first clue about the kind of wine that we can hope to obtain from the fruit harvested there. Grapevines absorb nourishment and behave differently according to the type of microenvironment where they grow. Chalky, clayey, or sandy soil, southern exposure to the sun, a breezy site where humidity is quickly dispelled: these sought-after elements vary from one vineyard to the next, giving varying results.

Of course, the variety of wine grape (a category quite separate from that of table grapes) also determines from the outset the kind of wine that will be produced.

Thus, the soil-climate combination and the grape variety are the two most important variables that explain the differences among wines.

It would be convenient to stop there and choose wine based only on the type of grape and the place of origin – Chardonnay from Languedoc, Niagara Chardonnay, Italian Chardonnay, and so on. After all, this already tells us a lot. But if it were as simple as that, wine wouldn't exercise such a remarkable power of attraction or excite so much passionate interest.

Many other variables have a determining influence on the quality of what you can expect to find in your wine glass: grapevine cultivation methods, the precise species of vine bought at the nursery (they vary in vigour and in resistance to certain threats; some adapt better to certain soils, etc.), the vinification technique and equipment – down to the type of yeast added in some cases, the type of oak in the barrels used for aging, etc.

Epitomizing the way each variable can make it mark, two wines made from Chardonnay grapes, both grown in the same plot on the same estate, cultivated by the same wine grower in the same manner, and which even have the same name and label, will taste quite different because of one detail: the small print on one of the labels says "aged in oak." Imagine then, how the difference is magnified when we compare wines from different vineyards, different wineries, different regions, or different countries, grown in different years with the inevitable differences in sunshine, rainfall, and temperatures.

Disconcerting? Admittedly. Challenging? Enormously. Obviously, time is needed to explore such a vast realm of possibilities. In any case, who ever said it was a good idea to try to learn everything there is to know about a particular subject in a few weeks? Curiosity is a cardinal virtue, but so is patience – in more than one respect – in the initiation to the marvellous pleasures of wine.

Connoisseurs complain that today, wines are starting to resemble each other too much – the curse of globalization – and they are not wrong in this. Nonetheless, the variety is still immense, and, for an inquisitive person who is not afraid of being caught unawares from time to time, gratifying surprises are legion.

How can we find our way when looking for good quality? Are there any general guidelines to point us in the right direction so that we can figure it out for ourselves, at least partially?

There are ways. Experienced tasters use certain indicators in a deduction-by-elimination process when guessing what a wine might be in a blind tasting. The same indicators can be used as guidelines when you're trying a new wine, or when you want to buy a good wine of a certain type. I refer to them frequently myself, and have included three of the major ones, below. (You may notice that price is not one of them!)

First indicator: Is it an Old World or a New World wine? In other words, is it of European origin, or does it come from California, Chile, or Australia? Depending on the climate, wine grown in the New World tends to be full-bodied, dark-coloured, juicy and fruity, and sometimes, mellow and fleshy compared to European wine.

French, Italian, German, and often even Spanish and Portuguese wines are distinguished by their high natural acidity and light body when compared to their New World equivalents. They are also less generous and velvety in character, and, it must be admitted, less captivating and accessible.

Of course, this is a sweeping generalization: we know how much microclimates or terroirs can differ within a region. There are also many exceptions for other reasons. But it is true that just knowing the wine's general geographical origin gives us our first clue about how it will taste.

Second indicator: The grapes used to make the wine. Producers may use a single grape variety, or combine them in assemblages – Cabernet-Syrah or Sémillon-Chardonnay blends, for instance.

New World wineries have always emphasized grape variety. "Varietal wines," that is, wines in which a particular grape variety predominates, are highly esteemed in their home markets, perhaps because consumers find them easier to understand; it's not hard to know what to expect from a wine that is labelled Merlot or Chardonnay.

In Europe, by contrast, the importance is given to the appellation rather than to the type of grape. Bordeaux, Burgundy, Rioja, Douro, and Chianti are all well-known, recognizable types of wine. On the other hand, Menetou-Salon, Jumilla, and Palmela are not. European wines (with appellations often being the only reference on the label) oblige us to put out our feelers and experiment to discover the aromas and flavours of little-known *crus*. The wine guides that are published annually, wine columns, as well as books and specialized magazines can be a big help in this respect.

Third indicator, and one which is increasingly becoming the ultimate reference, is the name of the wine grower, winery, or brand. Mondavi, Baron Philippe, Vineland Estate, Antinori, Torres, Guigal, Errazuriz, Trapiche: all of these are signatures which, although they don't necessarily guarantee the wine's superiority, minimize the risks of a letdown.

The list below contains the names of some of the major producers of wine widely available in North America that have shown an above-average reliability.

[Some Reliable Producers]

ARGENTINA Etchart, Trapiche, Catena, La Agricola, J.&F. Lurton.

AUSTRALIA Hardy's, Lindemans, Rosemount Estate, Jacob's Creek/Orlando, Penfolds, Peter Lehmann, Wolf Blass.

CALIFORNIA Mondavi, Beringer, Fetzer/Bonterra, R.H. Phillips, and Delicato.

CANADA Inniskillin, Vineland Estates, Jackson-Triggs, Cave Spring, Henry of Pelham, Konzelmann, Peninsula Ridge, Quails' Gate, Gehringer Bros, Mission Hill.

CHILE Errazuriz, Carmen, Tarapacá Ex-Zavala, Concha y Toro, Casa Lapostolle, Viña Casablanca.

FRANCE Hugel, Trimbach, and Cave de Pfaffenheim (Alsace); Duboeuf and Mommessin (Beaujolais); Jadot, Rodet, Laroche, Bichot, Drouhin, and Faiveley (Bugundy); Fortant/Skalli, Château de Nages, J & F Lurton, L'Hortus, Château de Valcombe, Domaine de Gournier, and Domaine de la Chevalière (Languedoc); Domaine Cazes (Roussillon); Guigal, Jaboulet, Cave de Cairanne, and Chapoutier (Rhône); Baron Philippe de Rothschild, Ginestet, and Domaines André Lurton (Bordeaux); Alphonse Mellot, Henry Marionnet, and Henri Bourgeois (Loire); Vignerons de Buzet, Union des producteurs de Plaimont, and Alain Brumont (Southwest).

ITALY Anselmi, Bolla, Maculan, and Masi (Veneto); Frescobaldi, Antinori, Rocca delle Macie, San Felice, and Banfi (Tuscany); Lungarotti (Umbria); Michele Chiarlo, and Pio Cesare (Piedmont); Taurino (Apulia); Fazi-Battaglia (The Marches); Sella & Mosca and Argiolas (Sardinia); Duca di Salaparuta and Tasca D'Almerita (Sicily).

PORTUGAL Sogrape, José Maria de Fonseca, Ferreira, and Aliança for table wines; Offley/Forrester, Graham, Taylor, Ferreira, Warre's, Niepoort, Delaforce, Infantado, Castelinho, Poças, Smith-Woodhouse, and Noval for port.

SPAIN Torres (Catalonia); Cosecheros y Criadores "Candidato" (Castile); Chivite, Conde de Valdemar, Montecillo, and Ijalba (Rioja); Real Sitio de Ventosilla "Prado Rey" (Ribera del Duero).

Low-cal Liqueur

"Port or Sauternes? *Do* tell me which one you want: I don't feel like playing at blind tasting tonight. Let's just say it gives me a headache."

"I can enjoy myself perfectly well without playing guessing games! But as you're kind enough to offer, I'd be happy with some tea, if it's not too much trouble. Well-steeped, if you don't mind. I like my Assam full-bodied and dark."

"Tannic, isn't that what you mean? Like Bordeaux used to be – that's what you went on about last time – how they would leave the juice soaking with the skins for weeks, even months, and how exciting it was in the old days..."

■ How is white wine made?

Pick some grapes in the vineyard and crush them. The juice that flows out will have almost no colour (even the pulp of red grapes is practically colourless). Pour the juice into a vat, and if necessary, add yeast to activate the fermentation process. After a few days, during which a few additional manipulations may be necessary, you will obtain "white" wine, that is, a pale straw-coloured, tanninless wine.

■ How is red wine made?

Proceed as for white wine, but don't separate the juice from the pulp right away. Crush the grapes as delicately as possible and leave the whole (the magma) to steep, like tea, for the juice to absorb the colour. The pigment is contained in the skins, not in the pulp (except in rare species called tinting grapes, whose pulp is also pigmented). The skins and juice are left together for a certain period of time to macerate (infuse); the must reddens as it is transformed into wine by fermentation. The result, as in any recipe, depends on the measurements and the ingredients, particularly the type of grapes used (some result in darker-coloured wine than others). Of course, the quality or type of wine desired by the wine grower, as well as the climatic conditions that year, also play influential roles.

■ And rosé?

Between white and red, rosé roughly corresponds to tea when the bag is dipped into hot water and removed a few seconds later. With its pale colour, it is the product of fermenting juice that has remained in contact with the skins for only a few hours. As soon as the desired tone is attained – pale pink, salmon, or dark pink – the juice is transferred, minus the skins, into another vat, and the fermentation process, already begun, continues.

As their maceration period is limited, rosés, even if some of them may be almost as dark as red wines, have very little tannins. Because of this, and because wine growers generally keep their best red grapes for making red wine, rosés are never great wines.

Pink champagne is exceptional, both in terms of quality and by the fact that much of it is a mixture of red and white wine – the only case allowed in the legislation concerning the elaboration of rosé wine – sparkling or still – in France, and if I'm not mistaken, in all of Europe.

[A Free Ride?

The tasting table is strategically placed right inside the entrance of the wine store. Behind a row of bottles, an employee, identifiable by his wine-coloured jacket, is assisting a stylishly dressed woman, who, at this moment, is sniffing wine in a glass, her eyes shut. The employee greets you and asks if you'd like to sample some white wine, and you learn that the elegant lady is the wine grower responsible for the product offered for your delectation. She leaves off her ecstatic assessment to give you more details.

"We're offering two Sauvignons from our vineyard in Western Australia – one aged in the barrel and the other unoaked. Which one would you like to try first?"

Seeing that you're in a quandary, she decides to come to your rescue, decreeing that ideally, you would begin with "the one that did time in the vat," to use her piquant expression.

"Oak is so sturdy and tough, don't you agree?" she adds, handing you a sample and winking at you.

Has this made things any clearer for you?

What is different about wines that are barrel-fermented or aged in casks, and are they really better because of it?

No, they are not better wines just for having been "raised" in wood. But what exactly are the meanings of expressions such as "barrel-fermented," "cask-matured," "aged in oak" (on French labels, *vieilli en fût, vinifié en barrique, élevé en foudre*), etc.? Simply that the wine has either been fermented (has passed from juice to wine) in wooden barrels or casks, or that, having been fermented in one manner or another, it has spent some time maturing in the barrel before being bottled and shipped to points of sale.

Ordinary ("bulk") wines may undergo the vinification process from crushing to bottling without ever coming into contact with wood. Much more likely, they are fermented and matured in huge stainless steel or cement-lined vats. Wine growers may decide not to ferment or age their wine in wood for economic reasons, or because they want the wine's characteristic bouquet to stay as pure as possible.

Contact with wood often imparts oak and vanilla flavours to wine, besides giving it a mellow, fat, creamy or buttery character. This can be an enhancement for a good wine. But for run-of-the-mill wines (that cost under $15, let's say), wood-aging can be oppressive and may mask the typical aromas and flavours of the dominant grape variety used. Overly wooded wines, whether they are made from Sauvignon, Chardonnay, or even Viognier grapes, strangely resemble each other, all of them exuding vanilla and pastry-cream aromas.

Here again, it's a matter of measurement and ingredients. The intrinsic quality of the wine-grower's product will determine whether oak, for wood-aging, or for fermenting in the barrel (the latter being a more gentle process than the former, bringing spicy, woody notes that integrate well with the wine) will be an ingredient or an expedient. In the latter case, a strong woody character may be intended to disguise the uninteresting nature or the poor quality of a wine.

What do you think of the increasing number of wine growers who add oak chips to wine that's fermenting in a steel vat to make it taste as if it were aged in the barrel?

This process, which gives the wine a barrel-aged taste at a fraction of the cost of the real thing, is carried out quite frequently, mainly in New World wine regions (Australia, California, Chile, Argentina, et al.) Producers do not necessarily mention this on the label. Their wines may still be perfectly good: again, it's a question of judging how much or how little oak is appropriate. There are even wine growers who drop whole oak planks into the vat, leave them for a certain number of hours or days, then remove it and carry on with the vinification process without thinking anything of it.

Such a crude method flies in the face of tradition and may set connoisseurs' teeth on edge, yet sometimes it can work quite well, producing well-balanced wines, without overbearing wood and vanilla notes.

Adding oak chips or planks may work, but doesn't aging in the barrel always make wine mature better, more naturally?

It does, without a doubt. Wood is porous and therefore "breathes." Oxygen also penetrates through the interstices of barrels – possibly more than through the wood itself. Thus, wine in a cask does not evolve in a completely hermetic environment. The tiny amount of air it receives through and between the barrel staves softens and ripens it as beneficial biochemical reactions take place. No such action occurs when oak chips or planks are submerged and left to steep in the vat.

The essential thing to know is that only better-quality wines, with sufficient character, body, and concentration, gain from an intimate association with wood. Furthermore, barrels are expensive: the best kind of oak barrel, which holds enough wine for about three hundred 750-ml bottles, costs over $1000.

An inventive shortcut is practised by some New World wine growers, for example, in Chile. In a technique called microbullage, tiny oxygen bubbles are injected into wine that already contains oak chips. This softens the tannins of a wine elaborated in a steel vat, and eliminates overly herbaceous notes. After this process, the wine is ready to drink as soon as it emerges from the vat, instead of having to spend a few months in a cask to obtain the same result – at least this is what the producers who employ this technique would have us believe.

But it says so right here in print!

"At the heart of our magnificent vineyards is an area blessed by the gods, where the vines benefit from an ideal microclimate, with optimum exposure to sunshine, excellent drainage, and the best sandy soil. Our talented oenologists bring all of their vast knowledge and passion to the making of this legendary wine of uncompromising quality, which will entrance you by its thrilling bouquet and tantalizing flavours. One sip and you too will fall under its irresistible spell. A sensory experience beyond compare."

Should we believe what's written on the back labels of wine bottles?

The text on the back of a wine bottle is essentially promotional hype. It's rather difficult to believe that we are about to uncork an absolutely divine nectar when the price sticker, still on the bottle, is marked $8.75!

Moreover, descriptions or comments on the labels of the best wines are usually very low-key. Although it would be stupid, from a commercial point of view, not to take advantage of the space offered by a back label to boast at least a little bit, where fine wines are concerned, the text is often limited to the bare facts – the grape variety, specifics of the vinification process, and, if the wine was aged in wood, the type of oak used and the length of time spent in the barrel.

Some back labels, however, even those of reputable wine growers and their representatives, tend to overdo it, including so many technical details that they look like lab reports. New World wineries are often guilty of this; American producers in particular like to display numbers. Instead of relying on poetics and tradition to carry the day, they seem to feel it's imperative to provide the alcohol rate to the second decimal (yes, some do this), the exact acidity rate, the Brix degree, etc.

On the whole, however, consumers are better off knowing too much than too little. Therefore, rapidly read over the back label – on which the producer has said whatever he or she felt like – to try to glean some practical, concrete information that will give you a better understanding of the wine you're thinking of buying or are about to drink.

It would definitely be useful, for example, to read that a white wine is "distinguished by its mellow and velvety character," by which you can conclude that it is probably rather sweet. This will certainly not please all of your guests, and above all, it will not be appropriate for an apéritif, when you normally want a wine that will stimulate the taste buds by its snappy acidity.

[Not Just Any Old Wood!

"Tonnellerie Chanson & Frères, bonjour! What can I do for you?"

"I'm calling from Canada. My brother-in-law makes his own wine and wins a lot of prizes every year..."

"I'm listening."

"A bunch of us got together and decided to buy him a barrel for his birthday. Can we order one from you and have it delivered to Canada? I can give you my credit card number."

"Just a moment, please. I'll have to check with our shipping department; your request is rather unusual. If I may be so bold as to suggest it, wouldn't you rather have a one-wine, or even a two-wine barrel? Here, we only deal in new wood."

"..."

"Are you still there? Please don't hang up! Perhaps you want new oak after all. However, we only use Allier, and occasionally, Vosges. Is that all right?"

Old barrels and new: what comes down in a second-hand barrel?

A "one-wine," or one-year barrel, has been used once: it has held wine for a determined number of months, was emptied and was probably reconditioned before new use, that is, scraped and charred to recreate the desirable smoke and toast flavours that new barrels impart to wine. A "two-wine," or two-year barrel, has held two successive vintages and has been reconditioned twice; the next wine that it will contain will not acquire much of a wood-aged taste. Nevertheless, this recycling can extend to a five-year period. The exceptions are the very large wooden vats called *foudres*, which can be used for centuries, as long as they are periodically repaired and reconditioned.

The main difference between old and new oak is that wine easily absorbs woody and vanilla aromas – sometimes quite strong ones – from a new cask. Only the best wines, highly concentrated, full-bodied and fruity from the start, can undergo this treatment without being overpowered. In the case of the above-mentioned homemade wine, as good as it may be, it is difficult to imagine that it could stand up to the effects of a drubbing by new oak.

In wine making, is French oak (the famous Allier, Vosges, and Limousin) really superior to the North American variety?

Even within France, no matter what cooperage methods are used to make the casks, wine has a distinctive taste depending on the region that the oak is from. Allier, Vosges, and Limousin oak each have distinctive characteristics that reflect their respective terroirs (the combination of microclimate and soil type).

Beyond these regional particularities, French oak is without a doubt a category apart. Many wine growers in different parts of the world consider it a point of honour to import (at huge expense) genuine French oak for the barrel-aging of their best wines, because of the subtle flavours that are absorbed from it.

American oak, on the other hand, imparts a stronger taste, sometimes described as a caramel flavour. The explanation for this is that the wood for the barrel staves is obtained by sawing instead of by splitting or cleaving along the grain as it is in France. Wood fibre that is severed by sawing imparts grosser, rougher notes to the wine.[1]

Another explanation for this difference in quality is that prime French oak is left to dry outdoors for a period of years before being used for casks. In the United States, where *vitesse oblige*, this process generally takes place in mechanized drying rooms in a fraction of the time.

Nevertheless, American oak has proved very successful with certain types of wine. In Spain, for instance, it has long been prized in vinification in the Rioja and Penedès regions.[2] Some wine growers try to obtain the best of all worlds by constructing hybrid casks, with the top and bottom of American oak, and the sides of French oak, although this may be a case of taking refinement to extremes.

Good barrel oak can be found in several other corners of the world: in Portugal, notably, as well as in the Balkans, Russia, and Canada.

---

1. A parallel can be drawn between this and the difference between European and North American cuts of meat: European cuts often have a more uniform tenderness because the direction of the fibre is respected.
2. American oak has even been seen in the orthodox Bordeaux region.

One Birthday Too Many

"Call me anything you want, but not 'old man!'"

"But you look terrific for your age!"

"Old schnook, old goat, old scag... whatever you like, but not, I repeat, not 'old man!'"

"What's the matter? Have you got something against your dad?"

What is meant by "old vines" in the wine industry?

The older a grapevine, the deeper its roots, and – in general – the better the taste and quality of its fruit. The deeper the roots grow (they can go down to ten metres underground), the more reliable and stable the vine's water supply will be. In times of drought, when the surface earth is dry and cracked, older vines easily find a good supply of water far below. The soil of the great vineyards – soil which is well-drained throughout the year – comprises the ideal environment for long-living vines.

In theory, and excluding a slew of other factors, wine made from old vines is of better quality and is more typical of its terroir. Generally speaking, young vines do not produce really good grapes until their third or fourth year, or "leafing." However, the phenomenon of wine being what it is, there are many exceptions to this rule. A three-year-old vine that has been radically pruned and restricted to bearing a very low number of bunches will produce quite acceptable grapes, sufficiently tasty and concentrated.

The problem for wine drinkers is that the qualification "old vines" on the label is not regulated at all: any producer can make the claim. This is not necessarily a reason to be suspicious of a wine so designated – the wine may indeed come from forty-year-old vines and be excellent. But you should be aware that the term is used loosely. Another point to consider is that "old" has different connotations in Europe, where quadragenarian vines are common, and in the New

World. In North America, grapevines planted ten or fifteen years ago are referred to as old; in this case, we can make a concession to the comparative youth of the wine industry here and let it pass.

How old can a vine be and still produce good wine grapes?

In general, a grapevine ceases to be productive after about fifty years. Again, there are numerous exceptions: in the Douro valley of Portugal, for instance, vines that are more than 120 years old continue to produce grapes – and what grapes! This particular piece of territory luckily escaped the phylloxera plague that wiped out practically all of Europe's vineyards at the end of the nineteenth century.[3] It produces the famous port, Quinta do Noval Nacional.

[Courtroom Dilemma

Setting: a courtroom, filled to capacity. A case that may create an important precedent in the field of wine and wine tasting is being heard.
Characters: the Defendants, "Tasters Anonymous," and the Claimants, "Drinkers Unlimited."
Act I, Scene 3:
The perplexed judge suddenly interrupts an impassioned plea by the attorney for the first party.

---

3. Phylloxera, the name of both the root-attacking disease and the aphid that spreads it, has never been totally wiped out. It reappeared in California at the end of the 1980s. As there is still no known antidote to it, the affected vines had to be destroyed, as they did many decades earlier, and thousands of acres were re-planted with stocks of phylloxera-resistant vines.

Am I to understand that all this fuss is because the parties dispute the use of the terms "tasting" and "drinking?" In my opinion, they are wasting the court's time!

Is there a difference between tasting and simply drinking wine?

The two are synonymous. The term "wine tasting" may seem pretentious in some circumstances, but the concept may help professionals and amateurs focus their attention (and sharpen their senses) in formal and informal wine-drinking contexts.

We could painlessly do away with truly pretentious synonyms for this activity, such as "sensory analysis," or "organoleptic examination," found in some books and promotional material.

This question is not quite an exercise in hair-splitting, if we leave the last word on the subject to Émile Peynaud, who says, in his masterful work, *The Taste of Wine*: "There is a great difference between drinking and tasting. Good wines and great wines are not drinks which are simply swallowed; one savours them."

In everyday life, however, it's perfectly all right to say: "We drank a magnificent Rioja last night." There's no profit in arguing over subtle differences in meaning. Drink it, taste it, savour it, imbibe it, quaff it – use any term you like. The important thing is to approach wine with neither fear nor favour, and wine, your faithful ally, won't let you down.

The Latest Scandal from France

You're waiting to board a plane in Paris and you decide to spend your idle time in the airport bookstore, with its international selection of newspapers and magazines. A front-page headline in a major French daily catches your eye:

"Domaine Mézoignon rejects appellation status!"

In the text of the article, this shocking statement by the wine grower is quoted:

> "In my conscience and in my soul, I prefer to stay with the *vin de pays* category. It's a better way of marketing my product. In any case, for what appellation status is worth... Our wine, which is neither fined nor filtered, doesn't need an appellation to appeal to customers."

Vin de pays; *appellation d'origine controlée*; *vin délimité de qualité supérieure*; *vino da tavola*; *indicazione geografica tipica*, etc. Is all this nomenclature really significant?

In Europe – not so much in North America and even less so in Australia – wine growers are subject to a stringent set of laws and regulations. Vintners cannot produce any kind of wine, anywhere, or in any way they like. And if they do not fully respect the legislation that applies in their region, they must declassify their wine and sell it under a less exclusive, less prestigious category, often at a lower price.

For example, if a passingly eccentric Bordeaux producer insisted on including a small amount of Syrah grapes (grapes from the corner of the estate with the best southern exposure) in his wine, he could go ahead and do this, but the wine could no longer be classified as Bordeaux. To remain in this particular *appellation d'origine contrôlée*, the wine would have to be made only of the grape varieties specified by law and tradition. For red Bordeaux, these are

Cabernet Sauvignon, Cabernet Franc, and Merlot, with smaller, accessory quantities of Malbec and Petit Verdot in some cases. Proportions are allowed to vary, but not the grape varieties.

How did this situation come about?

Partisans of the *appellation contrôlée* system say that it protects France's wine heritage. In other words, if wine labelled Bordeaux, Burgundy, or Côtes-du-Rhône could be made from any type of grape, serious confusion would result. Both specificity and typical character would suffer: wines that are theoretically quite different might end up tasting very much alike. The French above all, and other Europeans to a lesser extent, would risk losing their formidable competitive advantage over their New World rivals – who should not be underestimated from a marketing standpoint.

Detractors of the system concede that the regulations concerning the different appellations are solidly based on proven ancestral practices and experience. However, they feel that a greater flexibility in the rules would remove certain handicaps for European wine growers with respect to emerging wine-producing countries or regions.

A vigorous debate involving these opposing points of view continues to rage. Until a compromise solution is found, the consumer should know that it is becoming more and more chancy to rely on appellations when choosing wine. The name of the wine grower, estate, or company has become a better indicator of quality.[4]

Like vintage charts, official designations, appellations, and growth classifications only tell part of the story. A case in point: some Bordeaux château wines, classified as fifth growths (on a

4. Wine buyers have also begun to pay more attention to the names of the wine growers' representatives. This is especially – but not exclusively – pertinent with regard to the smaller agencies that propose wines to the different provincial liquor control boards in Canada. Some representatives specialize in certain regions or countries, promoting wineries whose products are either very typical or original in character.

scale of five), consistently outperform, according to general opinion, certain wines classified as second or third growths. This is notably true of the fifth-growths, Château Lynch-Bages and Château Pontet-Canet, which, for a few years now, have been more interesting than the second-growth Rauzan-Gassies or the third-growth La Lagune, in spite of the fact that all of these wines come from good terroirs.

Transferring our example to Burgundy, although a *grand cru* (great-growth, at the top of the quality scale) Chablis is superior, in principal, to a first-growth one, aberrations in the classifications occur in this region as well, resulting in bitter disappointments or – luckily – in magnificent surprises. In the case of a disappointing *grand cru*, we can conclude that even though its terroir is theoretically superior, the wine maker, for lack of talent or lack of means, was unable to bring out the wine's full potential.

I should emphasize again that, although the majority of classifications are not misleading, it's still safer to rely on the names of wine growers or châteaux for value and quality.

Does "unfined and unfiltered" on the label mean a better wine?

Fining is the addition of a substance to the wine in the barrel, vat, or tank that will bring all the suspended particles to the bottom. Egg white, gelatine, bentonite (a clay-like powder), and other products are commonly used, none of which will end up in the drinker's wine glass.

Even after fining, some kinds of wines need to be filtered mechanically if the wine maker wants a finished product that is brilliant and limpid, without a hint of turbidity. The wine passes through filters of varying degrees of porosity that will trap any remaining suspended matter, as well as any residual traces of yeast, thus stabilizing the wine and preventing it from refermenting in the bottle.

A few wine makers claim that fining or filtering wine thins it out, weakening its personality by taking away elements of its taste, along with the impurities. They prefer to market wines that may have a slightly cloudy appearance and visible sediment, reasoning that the wine is more natural that way.

There is no clear majority among those who are for or against fining and filtering in the vinification process. However, a consensus does exist that if fining and filtering are done, the vintner should go about it with a light touch, especially in the case of filtering.

[Rejection Letter

Dear Sir/Madam,

We regret to inform you that our organization is obliged to retract the Eco-Vinik certification from your vineyard.

Our inspectors recently discovered a large quantity of synthetic chemicals in the storage facilities at your winery. These products are incompatible with the making of a truly organic wine as we define it. In consequence, we must ask you to refrain from using any reference to our organization in labelling or promoting your wine, in your business correspondence, letterheads, etc.

We fervently hope that you will soon see the folly of your ways and take appropriate measures to be able to rejoin our association.

Yours sincerely,
Stretta Paraligna
Certification Committee
Eco-Vinik Inc.

Does truly organic wine exist, and does it taste any better in consequence?

Yes, it does exist, and above all, should not be confused with "biogenetic," or genetically modified wine. In France, 1% of the total wine production is certified organic; one third of it is grown in the Languedoc region. These wines, most of which are very good, are identified by the mention on the label: *vin issu de raisins de l'agriculture biologique* (wine made from organically cultivated grapes).

The main principle behind organic wine growing is the minimum use of chemicals with the maximum respect for nature and natural cultivation methods. Therefore, chemical herbicides, pesticides, and fungicides are replaced by natural methods to combat vine-ravagers like the grape-worm, with the ultimate goal of regenerating the soil by allowing normal bacterial activity to take place.

Organic wine growers use compost as fertilizer and either weed the vineyards mechanically, or allow the weeds to compete with the vines, stimulating them to push their roots deeper into the substratum to obtain their nourishment.

To control harmful insects, non-toxic techniques such as sexual confusion are applied. In this method, hormonal substances are spread onto the plants; this deregulates the parasites' reproductive cycle, and therefore, immediately diminishes their numbers. This type of intervention strengthens the vines together with their ecosystem, with the result that the vines are better able to resist attacks from various sources. Only Bordeaux mixture (a traditional copper-and-lime repellent against fungal diseases like mildew and oidium) and sulphur (see below) are allowed under organic certification.

Organic wine production, when it is done properly, has proved itself. There are few good vintners today who are not strategically reducing the use of chemicals in their production, trying to apply a balanced approach in the struggle against pests, weeds, and fungus.

They are well aware that the soil in many places has already been severely degraded and stripped of its vital micro-organisms.

Among the benefits of using organic methods in growing wine grapes is that, in general, their pulp is denser and their juice is more concentrated than that of their chemically assisted counterparts. If only because committed organic wine growers treat their vines and vineyards with care and respect, the vines respond in kind, and the wine made from them tends to have, if not a captivating taste, at least an authentic one.

There is a specific branch of organic farming called biodynamics, based on the theory of vital forces as developed by Austrian-born philosopher Rudolf Steiner in the first decades of the last century. As recently as ten years ago, ridicule was heaped on the "nutty" vintners who planned every stage of wine growing and vinification according to the conjunction of the planets and the movements of the Earth. "The Earth remains; we are only passing through" might be their motto, and encapsulates their attitude towards nature. Today, however, they are no longer the object of condescension. A pleiad of renowned wine-growing enterprises have adopted production methods based on biodynamics, and some of them display the famous "Demeter" seal on their labels. They include Coulée-de-Serrant (Loire), Château Romanin (Provence), Domaine Cazes (Roussillon), Kreydenweiss (Alsace), and Leroy (Burgundy).

Outside France – in the United States, especially – wine growers are eager to boast that their production is organic, but this is often without certification or other proof of their claims.[5] Of course, any product advertised as organic or natural has good market potential these days.

---

5. A notable exception: the Bonterra wines produced by the California company, Fetzer Vineyards.

Is sulphur harmful to the health? If not, why is the warning "Contains sulphites" mandatory on the labels of almost all wine sold in the United States?

Since sulphur is produced spontaneously during the fermentation process, all wine contains a certain amount of it, albeit a minuscule amount in some cases. Moreover, sulphur has been considered a necessary evil in wine making for centuries. It protects wine from oxidation and from undesired refermentation in the bottle. Even purists, like the adepts of biodynamics, use tiny doses of it.

Due to recent technological advances in wine production, a smaller quantity of sulphur than before is enough to make the important difference – although a crucial minumum is still indispensable and is likely to remain so. Used correctly, in measured doses, sulphur ensures that a wine destined for the marketplace is not only stable, but healthy.

Nevertheless, it is useful to know – especially if you are allergic to sulphur – that the lowest levels of it are found in red wines, followed by dry whites, then rosés, with the highest amount being found in non-fortified dessert wines (Sauternes, for example). The dose of sulphur needed roughly corresponds to the amount of sugar in the wine: the more sugar, the greater the chance that the wine will referment in the bottle, and therefore, the more sulphur required to prevent this.

In the Stars

You've picked a few cards at random from the well-shuffled pack. You're certain, however, that luck has nothing to do with it: you can feel a mysterious current between you and the cards, a current that is guiding your movements. Knowledge of the future is there for the asking.

No need to inform the fortune-teller that you're a wine lover: he's already read your mind. The cards you chose are hearts and clubs – the first evoking emotion and romance, the second, words and polemics.

A little pendulum swings to and fro to verify the exact time frames; then, your vital forces are recharged by means of crystals. The prediction can be pronounced: sooner than you think, you – and the rest of humanity with you – will have to be content with wine made from genetically modified grapes!

"But don't be upset," the soothsayer reassures you in a rush of sympathy. "None of the signs indicate that these wines will be anything but wholesome and delicious."

▌ Should we be wary of the advent of ▌ genetically modified wines?

First of all, they've practically arrived on the market already. Soon, we'll be able to buy wine made from vines that have been genetically modified to resist certain diseases, the cold, pests, etc. – the same inconveniences that have justified the creation of genetically modified corn, soy, and many other food products in North America. Based on our current state of knowledge, we cannot definitely affirm that we have suffered any deleterious effects from them. More to the point, however, what effects will show up ten, twenty, or thirty years from now? This is the essential question that no one can answer.

Attitudes on genetically modified food products vary. In Europe, people are generally circumspect, whereas in North America, there is little public awareness, and warnings are dismissed as alarmist by our politicians.

The genetic modification of a grapevine, like that of any other living organism, involves the introduction of a specific trait to give the species a property that it does not possess naturally. Besides vines, yeasts are also being genetically engineered so that they will secrete special enzymes and antibacterial agents.

For some time, wine growers have been using "designer" yeasts (not genetically modified as yet) to accentuate desirable characteristics in their wine. For example, Randall Grahm of Bonny Doon Wines in California readily admitted back in 1996 that he adds a particular yeast which enhances the fruitiness of his wines. In Canada, one of the best-known wine growers of the Niagara Peninsula has understandably expressed relief at the possibility of soon being able to plant new vine species whose resistance to the region's rigorous winters is due to genetic modification.

Our reticence towards this new technology is at its strongest when we are dealing with stem cell growth and reproductive cloning in the animal world, truly sensitive questions (a vine, on the other hand, as noble as it may be, is still a plant). It is usually an exercise in futility to try to stop "progress," but it doesn't necessarily mean that we have to allow an experimental free-for-all. In this sense, the ten-year moratorium on the marketing of genetically modified vines and wine requested in 2000 by Burgundian wine producers seems reasonable.

Nature vs. culture: to what extent do we human beings have the mandate to modify nature? And aren't we – with all our scientific advancements, but also with all our mistakes and delusions – part of nature too? Beyond the simple matter of discoveries in genetics, the major moral, philosophical, and even religious questions of our times reverberate in the world of wine.

Border Crossings

"You see?" ranted the driver. "When you cross the border, you notice the difference right away! The asphalt is suddenly as smooth as silk, there are no more potholes, and the white lines become visible. And they have exactly the same climate as we do; they use the same snow-plows and salt on the roads. How do you explain it, for crying out loud?"

"All right," the passenger imperturbably replied. "We have the same conditions, but maybe we don't take care of the roads as well as they do in the States. It's a matter of priorities, that's all. They invest more in their highways because they fantasize more about cars than we do. It's more of a status symbol for them."

"Maybe you're right about the roads, but what about the wine? How come they can make fantastic wines in New York State and we can't? Look at Ontario, even! I admit, it's colder in Quebec, but not that much colder. It freezes there too. Hell, it's the land of icewine!"

Why don't the different wine regions in Canada produce equally good wine?

This question is legitimate, since we know that great icewines, in demand all over the world, are produced in southern Ontario, only ten hours' drive from Montreal. But, although it's not far from the province of Quebec to the Niagara Peninsula, there is quite a difference in climate.

Even if much of Quebec and the Maritimes is in a more southerly latitude than the successful wine-growing areas of British Columbia (the Okanagan Valley, for example, is well above the 49th parallel), the climate is more extreme and the growing season is simply too short for the cultivation and elaboration of great wines, even of very good ones. Summer would have to be longer, beginning in early May and continuing until the end of October, instead of lasting from mid-June to September.

Pelee Island, one of southern Ontario's wine-growing regions, has a growing season that is an average of thirty days longer than that of the nearby mainland shore of Lake Erie. However, in spite of Ontario's climatic advantages, the majority of the best wines made there are white, since white grapes mature faster than red.

This last point also applies in Quebec and even in Nova Scotia, where good red wines are very rare – that is, red wines with the requisite colour, concentration, and fruitiness. The absence of an extensive period of warmth and sunshine prevents the grapes from fully ripening, and, like other fruit in the same environment, they lack sugar and remain acidic. Since good wine is the result of the transformation of sugar into alcohol under the action of yeast, it is understandable that unless the summer is very long and hot, especially during the crucial months of August and September, red wines made in Eastern Canada are almost always sharp, light-bodied, and acidic, with strong herbaceous notes reflecting the grapes' relative immaturity. Of course, one could always compensate (not to say cheat) by adding a packet of sugar to the vat, as is done quite often in France. However, a rise of more than 2 degrees in the alcohol rate makes for unbalanced wines that lack flesh and roundness, besides being overly alcoholic.

To produce fine white wines in Quebec, for example, high-quality grapes like Riesling, Chardonnay, Marsanne, Sauvignon, or Muscat would have to be cultivated on a large scale, in the open (i.e., not in greenhouses). However, the above varieties, even when the vines are covered by earth during the winter to protect them from the cold and the drying effects of wind chill, still do not bear sufficiently sweet, ripe grapes by harvest time: they need a lot more sun and heat. This is why cold-resistant hybrids and crosses such as Seyval and Vidal are resorted to – often with quite good results.

With global warming and advances in genetic research, who knows? We may soon develop a grape variety marvellously adapted to the colder regions of our country, a variety capable of producing a dry wine that will hold its own in world production.

Dreams do occasionally become reality!

■ What is icewine?

I cewine is made from the very sweet, very concentrated juice extracted from grapes frozen hard like marbles, crushed right after picking, outdoors, in the middle of winter (usually December or January). The temperature should be -8°C (17.6°F) or below, and should remain that cold over two or three days for the ideal harvesting conditions to be met.

The quantity of icewine made each year is very limited. In Southern Ontario, busloads of Japanese tourists often descend at the crucial moment to buy up almost the entire production. This is one reason for the rather exotic price of icewine ($50 for a bottle of the best Riesling-based type).

Icewine (from *eiswein*, developed in Germany in the eighteenth century) differs from other dessert wines like Sauternes and the *grains nobles* of Alsace because of its lower alcohol content (usually about 10%) and because it is often sweeter. Fortunately, it also has good natural acidity that livens it up and compensates for its syrupy texture.

On the other hand, icewine, whether it is from Ontario, British Columbia, Germany, or Austria, never possesses the complex bouquet and flavours of dessert wines made from grapes that shrivel on the vine before sub-zero temperatures set in. These grapes gain additional sweetness and concentration under the influence of noble rot (the desirable fungus *botrytis cinerea*), which gives the wine a range of other qualities, including unique aromas.

Icewine is also made in Quebec – for example, south of Montreal, in the vineyards of Dietrich-Jooss, Côtes d'Ardoise, and du Marathonien. The results are astonishing, and on occasion, rival the better Ontario icewines.

Blind Tasting Contest

An expectant silence reigned over the hall. It was the Canadian sommelier's turn on stage. She plunged her nose into her glass again and again, her eyes closed, continually sloshing the wine around as if prey to a nervous tic.

"Madam, you have one minute and thirty seconds left. Can you give the jury your opinion on the kind of wine you are tasting?"

"I don't need any more time," snapped the contestant, opening her eyes. "Nothing is gained by overdoing it. I prefer to go with my first impression."

"A wise decision," the moderator could not help commenting.

"Here we go, then: there's honey, a mineral element, and something like chalk, I'd say. So, I'll opt for a Loire Valley white, Chenin Blanc, a recent vintage."

"Touché! You've hit it right on the nose! It's a 1999 dry Domaine Huet Vouvray! Congratulations!"

The audience applauded wildly, thrilled by the excellent showing of their hometown favourite – all except a doubting Thomas sitting near the back, who elbowed his neighbour and wisecracked: "Sure – she can smell honey, chalk, and rocks in a glass of wine! What else? Tar, sheep manure, and oysters maybe?"

How can wine, made exclusively from grapes, smell like chalk, roses, or raspberries?

This is possible because the naturally occurring chemical and molecular constituents of wine form an almost infinite number of volatile components that are detectable by our sense of smell. It may seem like a sleight of hand, but it's more or less the same phenomenon as the flavours in "tropical fruit" chewing gum, which doesn't contain an atom of real mango, papaya, or pineapple. The company's lab technicians have isolated an aroma molecule found in one or another of those fruits, reproduced it synthetically, put it into the gum, and presto!

Of course, wine producers do not inject flavours into their wine. The aroma molecules are present as if by enchantment, partly drawn from the soil that nourished the vines, and partly formed by the multifarious chemical reactions that occur when the must ferments into wine. To give just one illustration, the aroma of green pepper that we can sometimes smell in Cabernet Sauvignon is due to the presence of the 2-methoxy-3-isobutyl pyrazine molecule.

When wine matures, either in the cask or in the bottle, its aroma molecules do not disappear: they change. They reorganize into new groupings, causing new volatile components to emerge. At this point, when we smell the wine, it will present a whole new range of aromas. This is one of the main reasons that wine is said to be alive: it is continually transforming itself.

By the middle of the twentieth century, scientists had discovered, isolated, and identified about fifty substances responsible for as many aromas in wine. Now, at the beginning of the twenty-first century, technology has made it possible to detect nearly a thousand different aromatic compounds!

This proves that the professional taster who claims to detect three or four aromas that not only have distinct characteristics but are outright exotic may not be exaggerating at all. Furthermore, although the human nose cannot compete with today's sophisticated technology in objectivity and precision, it can't be beaten when it comes to sensing a wine's finesse and "race," in other words, whether it is an aristocrat or a plebeian, notwithstanding its aromatic qualities.[6]

You've probably wondered about the odd fact that wine almost never smells of grape juice. In effect, fermentation irreversibly transforms the characteristics of the juice of all grape varieties, with the

---

6. Even perfumers, who must have the best-attuned noses in the world, are only capable of distinguishing four or five odours in the one perfume. Thus, wine tasters do not come off too badly in this contest of smelling skills.

exception of the Muscat grape of the south of France. Muscat, the most aromatic of all wines, is also one of the least complex, and the one with the least number of aromas... other than that of fresh Muscat grapes.

Picking the Champions

Ladies and gentlemen: in this corner, weighing 75 kilos, we have Phil "Sunny Boy" Petrus, the fastest grape-picker in the world. He's tanned and muscle-bound, but he's got the delicate fingers of a pianist! His basket is strapped on his back, ready to receive the sun-gorged grapes that he's going to pick, vine by vine, as soon the gong sounds.

In the opposite corner, shiny, oiled, cranked up and ready to go, the challenger, Miss Grape-Harvesting Machine. Let her loose in the vineyard for half an hour and she'll pick more grapes than twenty prime human beings can pick in half a day!

Is there any difference in taste between a wine made from grapes harvested by machine and one made from grapes picked by hand with a trusty pair of grape shears?

We have to look at the way a mechanical harvester works to understand its advantages and disadvantages. It's a kind of adapted tractor that passes alongside a row of vines, straddling the vines as it goes. Lateral bars shake the stalks, and the ripe grapes fall onto a conveyor belt and roll into large containers.

The obvious advantage of the mechanical harvester is that it can collect a huge amount of grapes in record time. This rapidity is crucial when rain, which may dilute the juice of the ripe grapes, is forecast. The machine can be used at night (as it is in Australia) to collect the grapes when they are cooler. It is also a godsend if manpower is lacking at harvest time. As you might imagine, a harvesting machine costs a small fortune. Wine growers often go halves on one, or rent it out to their colleagues – unless they own very large vineyards, in which case it is profitable for them to have their own exclusive harvester.

The main inconvenience of the mechanical harvester is that, even when a blower is strategically mounted over the conveyor belt, a certain amount of unripe grapes, twigs, leaves, stems, and even insects roll into the bins together with the ripe grapes. The ideal way to prevent these unwelcome bits and pieces from conferring unpleasant vegetal and herbaceous notes to the wine is to have an additional checkpoint, a sorting table with a slow conveyor belt, for example, where workers can pick over the gathered produce before it enters the winery.

There are other disadvantages to the mechanical harvester. Shaking the vines weakens them and shortens their productive lifespans. The gas-operated vehicle inevitably pollutes the air in and around the vineyard. Also, to accommodate the mastodon harvester, the vines must be planted farther apart than in vineyards where the grapes are hand-picked, which may result in less concentrated juice. Last but not least, mechanical harvesting eliminates the team spirit and camaraderie that has been a pleasant, traditional aspect of grape harvesting through the centuries.

Most of the ordinary wine available in North America is made from machine-picked grapes.

Hand-picking, often done by women, who are reputed to be more nimble-fingered and discriminating in their work than men, remains the preferred method at almost all the prestigious châteaux. Whether traditional hand-picking is done to maintain a certain image associated with the established quality of the wine (this may also explain why some producers hesitate to replace natural cork) or for other, more practical reasons, the fact remains that no machine will ever equal the human hand, and especially not the human eye for finding and picking only grapes that are at their peak, even if this implies a return visit to the vineyard a few days later. While the harvesting machine essentially brings single grapes to the winery, pickers choose bunches of grapes that are as ripe as possible. The stems are removed afterwards by a de-stemming machine, although must is rarely 100% free of MOG (material other than grapes).

In some vineyards, hand-picking may be the only option. For Sauternes, only the bunches displaying noble rot are picked, implying several visits to the vineyard. In many vineyards, the terrain is too steep for machine harvesting; manufacturers claim that harvesters can be used on 30-degree-angle slopes, but this is only possible when the ground is reasonably even.

Some grape varieties are known to suffer from the ungentle effects of mechanical picking, for example, Pinot Noir and Grenache. The vine species used in the Bordeaux appellations, on the other hand, have been found to stand up quite well to mechanical harvesting.

In conclusion, human expertise in this domain is preferable by far. However, this incontestable fact should not make us prejudiced against some of the excellent wines that are made from machine-picked grapes.

The Call of the Wild

The trunk and back seat of the car overflowed with camping paraphernalia: sleeping bags, a tent, baseball mitts, rubber boots, sandals, clothes, a propane stove, plastic utensils, food, etc., etc.

"Nicky, we said no wine this time! This case takes up too much room: you'll have to leave it here."

"But there's only red in it!"

"What difference does that make?"

"Hmm... how can I make you understand? You insisted on bringing the first aid kit, didn't you? Four days in the bush without my daily dose of Bordeaux, with *my* hereditary tendencies, before you know it, it'll be goodbye to camping trips and hello to the I.C. unit and the I.V. hookup. I'm only taking basic precautions!"

Is anyone still skeptical about the marvellous health benefits of regularly drinking red wine?

Yes: *I* am. But let's go back to the beginning of the 1990s, when the Americans discovered what they called "the French paradox."

Many French citizens consume large quantities of fat, smoke cigarettes, and have sedentary lifestyles. Even so, their rate of heart disease is considerably lower than that of North Americans. One explanation for this is that the French eat more fresh fruit and vegetables than we do, but the other, more glaringly obvious difference is that they drink more red wine. Drunk regularly, slowly, and moderately (1/4 bottle per person, per day), ideally with meals, red wine cleanses the arteries. It lowers the rate of bad cholesterol in the blood, besides having antioxidant properties.

Studies confirming these findings have appeared in medical journals almost monthly since they were first "discovered." (Actually, Dr. Masquelier, a pharmaceutics professor at the University of Bordeaux, had already observed, tested, and proclaimed the cholesterol-busting power of wine in 1961.)

The nuance that should be brought to this question, besides the fact that the French face other types of diseases related to their diet and lifestyles, is that practically all scientific studies are eventually disproved, contradicted, or qualified to a certain extent. Thus, researchers have warned that the observed correlation between red wine consumption and good blood circulation is not necessarily a matter of cause and effect. They also remind us that the incidence of other diseases (cancer and digestive and neurological problems) increases with the consumption of alcohol, even in very small quantities.[7]

A recent Scandinavian study suggests that it may not be the red wine and tannins themselves that account for better cardiac health, but rather the healthier and more active lifestyles that are practised by regular wine drinkers in Scandinavia, Canada, and the United States.

There's no point in depriving yourself of the immense pleasure of drinking your favourite Côtes-du-Rhône, Bardolino, or Zinfandel. For many reasons, wine is good for the body as well as the soul, although we shouldn't necessarily tout it as a cure-all.

A Succession... of Misfortunes

It was a momentous find: after hours of rumaging through our dear-departed Great-uncle Henry's wine cellar, my cousin and I came across three bottles of 1955 Château Grand-Puy Lacoste, a Bordeaux made in the *commune* of Pauillac. That very evening, trusting – too much, perhaps – in our ancestor's oenological knowledge and good taste, we made a ceremony of opening one of the bottles. In solemn and eloquent silence, we poured and tasted. The wine wasn't bad; it still had some fruit, but what acidity! Perhaps there had been storage problems? Not very likely: Uncle Henry always knew exactly what he was doing as far as wine was concerned, and always kept his cellar in good condition. Maybe it was a fluke. We decided to try a second bottle.

The wine in it was the same as the first, perhaps even more acidic. And the third one was just as – I'll say it, even though it hurts –

---

7. See www.eurocare.org/profiles/franceparadoxfrench.htm

vinegary. Curiously, the level of the wine in the bottles had been promising, and the colour, though leaning towards orange, was still red enough.

"The worst of it is," my cousin philosophized, "that we'll never know if it was a great wine gone bad, or if it had always been bad."

▌Does wine made these days taste the same as wine made thirty, forty, or fifty years ago?

No, it doesn't. Tastes evolve and change, and today, we would find it difficult to appreciate what was considered good wine in the middle of the last century in Europe, for example. Most red wine made then was acidic and tannic. The best wines of that epoch – the ones that were made in very warm years – have come down to us relatively unspoiled. They are usually so concentrated that their flavour compensates for their sharpness. However, they are the exceptions. If we go back still further in time, most ordinary wine bore a dangerous resemblance to vinegar. It was acrid and harsh, and was meant to be drunk within the year.

Over the last forty years, the science of oenology, and vinification technology with it, have made huge strides. We know much better where we are going in wine making. Fermentation and barrel-aging are carried out with greater precision and predictability, and it is no longer so risky for vintners to wait until their grapes are at the peak of maturity before beginning the harvest.[8]

8. It is less certain, however, that the great wines of today will show the same staying power as their predecessors. Twenty years has been the approximate age limit for the vast majority of dry wines made in these last few decades (unless they are fortified, like port). However, this too is a matter of taste: as mentioned earlier, the British are being notoriously fond of older wine that might seem thin and practically in decline to us North Americans. We need more time and experience to have a better idea of the aging potential of the fine wines produced using the full advantages of modern technology.

Even ordinary wines – especially ordinary wines – have benefited from technological progress. Softer, rounder, and fruitier than in the past, their full range of aromas and flavours can be appreciated as soon as they are on the market.

To have a balanced picture of the present situation, we should remember that, like fashions, tastes change and go out of style. If we had served a dry white wine of today to guests from Bordeaux at the beginning of the 1900s, they probably would have spat it out in disgust, having found it thin and acidic. In those days, almost all white wines contained the natural sweetness of grapes. People preferred them like that, and with this in mind, vintners left the grapes on the vine as long as possible, usually until late November. Then again, it might have been the other way around, with the customary wine-growing procedures giving a fairly predictable result and people adapting their expectations to it. As is probably also true today, they liked a particular taste because that was what they were accustomed to.

Whatever the case, one thing is certain: wine growers the world over are now immeasurably more in control of their production than in the past. With better results, even if nature – the climate, the soil, and certain other imponderables – continues to add its pinch of salt to the recipe.

▌Wasn't wine, Bordeaux for one, less alcoholic in the old days?

T his is true. As recently as the early 1980s, the alcohol rates of many red Bordeaux hovered around 11.5%. They stealthily edged higher over the years, and today, alcohol rates of 13% and even 13.5% are not uncommon. Increasingly, wine growers plan their harvest to select the ripest grapes; optimal maturity is sought more for fruitiness than for sweetness, and, whenever possible, for ripe tannins. The ripest grapes being the sweetest, they necessarily give the wine a high volume of alcohol, if no residual sugar is to be left at the end of the vinifcation process – in which case, red wine would end up tasting sweet instead of dry.

Chaptalization (the addition of sugar at the start of the fermentation process) produces the same effect, pushing the alcohol rate up. It is resorted to more and more frequently.

Why is this? Wines with a high alcohol content are usually fat and velvety, with a glycerine-laden charm that makes them appealing at first sip, although, in several of them, accessibility and sweetness take away from finesse and freshness.

With wine, as with everything, we quickly grow tired of nourishment that lacks spiritual substance...

[Selected Bibliography]

I t would have been impossible to write this book without consulting innumerable other books, as well as magazines and web sites. This was done sometimes with alacrity, sometimes with discouragement, since, in this domain, it frequently happens that the sources contradict each other or lead in opposite directions. My task was to sort out an overabundance of information, separating the true from the false to the best of my ability, reaching definite conclusions whenever possible, but often having to point out that certain questions remain unresolved.

Among the many reliable texts that allowed me to corroborate facts and reveal little-known aspects about the world of wine, I have selected the ones that stayed open on my desk almost constantly and were the most useful during my research for this book.

They would constitute a good core library for a wine enthusiast – you, perhaps – who has mastered the basics and is thirsting for deeper knowledge.

Books

Alexis Lichine's New Encyclopedia of Wines and Spirits, Alfred A. Knopf, 1985.

ASPLER, Tony, *Vintage Canada*, 3rd edition, McGraw-Hill Ryerson, 1999.

CASAMAYOR, Pierre, et al., *The Hachette Wine Guides*, Cassell Illustrated, London.

DRAPEAU, Pierre, and André VANASSE, *The Encyclopedia of Home Winemaking, Vol. 1.: Fermentation and Winemaking Methods*, Pendulum Press, Montreal, 1998.

EWING-MULLIGAN, Mary, and Ed MCCARTHY, *Wine for Dummies*, 2nd edition, Hungry Minds, 1998.

HALLIDAY, James, and Hugh JOHNSON, *The Vintner's Art – How Great Wines Are Made*, Simon and Schuster, 1992.

Hugh Johnson's Pocket Wine Book, Mitchell Beazley, 2003.

Oz Clarke's Introducing Wine: A Complete Guide for the Modern Wine Drinker, Harcourt Brace & Co., 2000.

PEYNAUD, Émile, *The Taste of Wine: The Art and Science of Wine Appreciation*, 2nd edition, John Wiley & Sons, 1996.

PEYNAUD, Émile, and Alan F.G. SPENCER, *Knowing and Making Wine*, John Wiley & Sons, 1984.

STEVENSON, Tom, *The New Sotheby's Wine Encyclopedia*, Dorling Kindersley Ltd., 1997.

In French

BENOIT, Jacques, *L'art de la dégustation*, La Presse, Montreal, 2000 (eight booklets).

DOVAZ, Michel, *Dictionnaire Hachette du Vin*, Hachette Pratique, 1999.

SENDERENS, Alain, *Le vin et la table*, Éditions de la Revue de vin de France, 1999.

Magazines

Decanter
Gambero Rosso
Harpers
Wine Access
Wine Magazine
Wine Tidings

In French

L'Amateur de Bordeaux
Gault Millau
Le Point – Spécial Vins
La Revue de vin de France
Vins & Vignobles

Tasting Newsletters

Burghound.com (exclusively about Burgundy; Allen Meadows)
International Wine Cellar (Stephen Tanzer)
The Vine (Clive Coates)
The Wine Advocate (Robert Parker)

Some good Internet sites

www.enology.net
www.finewinediary.com
www.ivinum.com
www.jancisrobinson.com
www.tastings.com
www.tonyaspler.com
www.wine-pages.com
www.wineanorak.com
www.wineloverspage.com
www.winemega.com
www.wineserver.ucdavis.edu

In French

club.amis.vins.free.fr
http://crus.classes.free.fr/glossaire_vigne.htm
www.abrege.com/lpv/index.htm
www.crusetsaveurs.com
www.lescaves.qc.ca

[Index]

A

acidity: and aging (red, white), 21, 119, 123; basic taste sensation, 12, 86; of Canadian wine, 163; and decline, 128; desirable in whites, 21, 36; of European wine, 137; and food, 61, 81, 86, 125, 147; getting used to it, 61; higher rates in past, 172; in icewine, 164; and sweetness, 99 (footnote)

age of wine, determining peak, 21; indicated by colour, sediment, 16, 123

aging: accelerated, 62, 72, 145; aging potential indicators, 21, 116, 123, 128, 129, 172; aroma transformation, 16, 128, 129, 166; benefits, 16; in half-bottles, 115; humidity desirable during, 108; and majority of wines, 115, 144; method determines result, 136, 144; wood aging, 143-145, 147-149. *See also* cellar; barrels; evolution; oak

Aglianico (S. Italy), red, aromas, 43; cellar suggestion, 119

air: permeability of corks, 25, 26, 104, 105, 108; sucking in when tasting, 13

airing wine: and aromas, 64; breathing in bottle, 57, 61, 62; decanting, 21, 71, 72; microbullage, 145; softens tannins, 21, 57, 62, 72

alcohol: alcoholic taste, 17, 54; degree in rosé (high = dry), 80; health risk, 171; high degree diminishes freshness, 174; higher rates in recent years, 173; increased by chaptalization, 99, 163, 174; in port, 59, 108; prevents oxidation, 105

Alsace, Alsatian wine: and appellations, 138; aromas, 42, 49; with asparagus, cheese, sauerkraut, 81, 83; biodynamic wine, 158; half-bottles for cellar, 115; with oriental and spicy food, 89; reliable producers, 139. *See also* Riesling; Sylvaner; *grains nobles*

Amarone (Veneto): red cellar suggestion, 119; evolution, 127; with Gorgonzola, spicy food, 81, 89

analogy (in describing wine), 34, 38, 48

animal (game) aroma, 39, 42, 43, 48

aniseed based liquors, 85 (note)

anosmia, 5

antibacterial agents: in genetically modified yeasts, 161

antioxidant properties of wine, 170

apartment cellars, 110, 111

apéritif wines: freshness, preservation after opening, 58, 59; with hors d'oeuvres, 85; New World whites, 61, 147

appellations, 16, 20, 124; *d'origine contrôlée*, 153-155; greater significance in Europe, 138; less significant than names of vintners, 138, 154, 155

Apulia (S. Italy) reds: aromas, 43; cellar suggestions, 119; reliable producers, 140

Argentine wines, 83, 89; reliable producers, 138, 139

aromas, 10-13, 19, 41, 35, 48, 49, 164-166; complexity of, 20, 164; detecting, naming, 39, 40, 44, 45, 166; fade with oxidation, 35, 57, 128; getting used to, 11; and glassware, 21, 64-66; major categories, 40, 41, 44, 45, **Table**, 41; multiplicity of, 11, 37, 39, 41, 166; nose's discriminating powers, 40, 166; in old wine, 11, 16, 48, 123; practice kits, 49; released in glass, 64, 65, 96, by swirling, 10, 64, 65; tip for detecting several, 44, 45; transformed by fermentation, 166; typical, of certain wines, **Table**, 42, 43; unidimensional, 128, 129; of young wine, 16, 123, 128, 129. *See also* individual aromas and aroma categories; odours; wine tasting

aromatic persistence, 13, 25

assemblages, 138; Australian, 120; Bordeaux, 153, 154

astringency, 46; desirable in red, white, 21; in Italian wine, 17. *See also* acidity; tannins

attitudes, New World vs. European: age of vines, 150, 151; age of wine, 123; crystals in wine, 99; genetically modified products, 160; use of freezer, 54

Australia, Australian wines, 137, 143, 144; Cabernet/Shiraz blend, cellar suggestion, 120; dessert wine cellar suggestion, 121; night harvesting in, 168; reliable producers, 139; Shiraz, evolution, 127; whites as apéritif wines, 61

B

balance, in mouth, 12; necessary in aging, 21

Bandol (S. France): red, white cellar suggestions, 118; white, rosé with bouillabaisse, 83

Banyuls (Roussillon): with dessert, chocolate, 88; dessert wine cellar suggestion, 120; maple syrup aroma, 49

barrels: aromas imparted by, 24, 143-145, 148; construction, 148, 149; expense, 143, 145, 147; fermenting in, 143, 144, 172; hybrid, 149; oak, 136, 143-145, 147-149; reconditioned and new, 147, 148; and variety in wine, 143, 148, 149. *See also* aging in wood; oak

Beaujolais, 17; aromas, 43; cellar suggestion, 117; with Eastern European, Greek food, 90; evolution, 126; pale, light-bodied, 10, 17, 54, 80; reliable producers, 139; with roast chicken, oysters, 83, 86

Beaujolais nouveau: colour, 10; when to drink, 126

biodynamics in viticulture, 122, 158, 159

bitterness (basic taste sensation), 12

bizarre, unpleasant, **aroma category**, 41

blind tasting, 12, 15-18, 21, 46, 165; snares in, 16

body: definition, 34; full-bodied, 20, 34, 80, 87, 98. *See also* robustness, flavour

Bordeaux region and wines, 79; alcohol rates, 173, 174; appellations and grape varieties, 153, 154; best reds, whites, evolution, 126; châteaux and classified growths, 16, 107, 154, 155; great Bordeaux, mute phase, 129, 130; half-bottles for cellar, 115; mixture (anti-fungal solution), 157; red, with lamb, 83; reliable producers, 139; typical character, 17, 42, 138; University of, 66, 170; use of American oak, 149; white with shellfish, chicken, 86, 87

bottles: leave on table for inspection, 72; opening, ritual aspect, 26;

Chinon (Loire): cellar suggestion, 118; red, with fish, 79

chips, oak, 144, 145

chocolate: with port or Banyuls, 88; clashes with wine, 88

"Christmas tree" drainer stand, 73, 74

clarity of wine, 10, 71, 72, 123, 155, 156

classified growths: 16 (definition), l07, 127, 138, 154, 155; evolution, 127; first growths, 16, 122, 155; *grands crus* (great growths) 16, 19, 26, 28, 132, 155; ranking, 154, 155

climate: in Canada, 162, 163; importance in wine growing, 12, 72, 124, 135, 136, 162, 163

coffee, 7, 34, 41, 81, 88

colour of wine, 10, 14, 163; affected by oxidation, 35; darker with dark meat, 80, 87; enhanced in decanter, 72; indicates alcohol rate in white, 34; indicates evolution, age, 16, 123, 128; paleness of Beaujolais, 10, 17, 54; related to aroma, 44; related to flavour concentration, 34; related to food, 80, 98; in vinification process, 141, 142

complexity: of great wine, 20; loss of, 128; of Sauternes, 164

components of wine, 109, 128; aromatic, molecular, and volatile 55, 66, 109, 165-167; flavour, 156

concentration, 17, 23, 116, 150, 163, 164, 168, 172; in viticulture (extract), 124

cooked fruit aroma, 128

cooling wine. *See* chilling

corks: cracked, fissured, 95; dried, shrunk, 104, 108; natural more prestigious, 168; permeability, 25, 26, 104, 105, 108; pieces in wine, 69; presenting at restaurants, 95, 96; re-use for leftover wine, 56; smell of, 95, 96; synthetic, 26, 104, 105; wax tabs on, 104; wine-soaked end ("mirror"), 56, 95

corked wine, 35 (definition); causes, 24-26; damp odour, 35; detecting it, 23, 24, 94-96, 100; dry, thin taste, 24, 35, 95; remedies, 25, 26;

statistics, 25; taste, 24; trichloranisole (TCA), 25, 26

corkscrews, 67, 68

cost of wine: icewine expensive, 121, 164; quality/cost ratio, 20, 107, 146; splurging for special occasion, 70; of stocking cellar, 106, 107, 113, 114

Côtes-du-Rhône, 116, 171; appellations, 154; red, with beef, 83; white with steak tartare, 87, 98. *See also* Rhône Valley wine

Crozes-Hermitage (Northern Rhône), 39, 114; red cellar suggestion, 117

crus (growths), 16 (definition), 19, 28, 122, 138. *See also* classified growths, *grands crus*

crystal wine glasses: cost, 63; damaged by dishwater, 67; decanters, 71; lead content of, 73

crystals (tartaric): in bottle, 99; acidity/sweetness relation, 99 (footnote)

D

decanters, decanting, 71-74; cleaning, 73, 74; crystal 71, 73; draining, drying, 73, 74; softens tannins, 21, 62, 71, 72. *See also* airing wine; colour of wine

decline of wine, 123, 128, 129, 171, 172; in cellar, 108; port, 59

decomposing vegetation aroma (Burgundy), 11, 42, 48

descriptive terms, 33-40, 44-49; short-cut descriptions 33-36, 44; use of analogy, 34, 38, 48

dessert wines: cellar suggestions, 120, 121; and cheese, 88; crystals in, 99 (footnote); evolution, 127; with food, 81, 82, 88; fruitiness, 59, 121; late harvest, 121; preservation after opening, 58, 59; serving temperature, 53; sulphur in, 159; versus icewines, 164

determining peak readiness, 21, 115, 122-130. *See also* evolution

diluted taste, 13; by rain, 124, 168

Douro (Portugal): phylloxera-free region, 151; port, 151; red cellar suggestion, 126; robust reds, evolution, 127; typical character, 138

drainage (soil), 124, 150

dried-out taste: in corked wine, 24, 35, 95; in wine in decline, 16, 128

dryness: dry before sweet rule, 60, 61, 85; indicated on labels, 82, 80; and sweetness in white, 34; and tannins, 36

E

effervescence, 59; in Champagne, 68, 69

Europe vs. New World: appellations more important, 138; more laws and regulations, 153, 154, 158; wines lighter, more acidic, 137. See also attitudes

evolution of wine, 21, 108, 122-130, 166: **Table**, 126, 127

F

fermentation, 141, 142, 163, 166; in barrel, 143, 144; techniques better today, 172

filtering and fining wine, 72, 155, 156

fine wine:16, 54, 126; with cheese, 80

finish. See aromatic persistence; length.

first impression in tasting, 11, 46, 47

fish and wine, 79, 82, 83, 86, 98

flavours, 166; complex in great wine, 20; fruity in red wine, 35; molecules in wine, 156; oak, 144; strong, 33, 34, with food, 80, 87; thin, 16, 24, 35; unidimensional when wine in decline, 128, 129. See also tastes

floral aromas, 39, 41-44, 46; **aroma category**, 24, 41

food and wine matches, 77-90, 93, 94, 97, 98, 114; cheese: enemy of wine, 80, better with white, 61, regional wine and cheese pairings, 81, 88; desserts, 81, 82; fish, shellfish, 79, 80, 82, 83, 86, 98, 135; food attenuates acidity, 61, 125; hors d'oeuvres and dry whites, 147; interdictions, 82, 85; meat, 77, 78, 80, 83, 87, 97, 98; national combinations, 89, 90; traditional pairings, 82, 83; two different approaches, 77-79, 83; wine with

types of food: **Table**, 85-88; world cuisine and wine: **Table**, 89, 90; variables, 84

fortified wine: protected from oxidation, 105, 172. See also port

France, French wines, 63, 142, 148, 149; biodynamic wines, 158; French paradox, 169-171; reliable growers, 139; wine laws, 153-155; wines for cellar, 117, 118, 120. See also Alsace, Bordeaux, Burgundy, etc.

freezer: for cooling wine, 54; for conserving wine, 57 (footnote)

fresh muscat aroma, 35, 166, 167

freshness: and acidity, 128; and alcohol rate, 174; of apéritif wines, 58, 59, 85; evolution: **Table**, 126, 127; and light, temperature, 103, 108; preservation after opening bottle: **Table**, 58, 59; of restaurant house wine, 97

fruit, fruitiness: of apéritif, dessert wines, 58, 59, 85, 121; **aroma category**, 24, 41; in aromas and flavours, 24, 35, 39-44, 48, 123, 128, 165, 166, **Table**, 41-43; and climate, 163, 172; and colour, 44; and decline, 108, 128; definition, 35; and designer yeast, 160; desirable in wine, 24, 25, 59; doesn't mean sweet, 35; greater than in past, 173; of New World wines, 17, 98, 137; and oak, 148; and oxidation, 35, 59; relation to temperature, 54, 108; of young wines, 16, 123

full-bodied: use of term, 34. See also body; robustness

fungus (mildew, oidium), 157

G

gasoline odour in wine, 42, 48

genetically modified vines and yeast, 9, 160, 161, 163

German wine: Auslese with lamb, 97; cellar suggestions, 119; icewine, 164; longevity, 119; with spicy food, 89; sweet white with cheese, 88

Gewurztraminer (Alsace): aromas, 42;
with Munster cheese, 81; with
Oriental food, 89

Gigondas (Southern Rhône), 38; red
cellar suggestion, 117, 118;
evolution, 127

glasses (wine): how to hold, 65; pouring
level, 14, 64, 65; seasoning, 64;
storing, 64; swirling technique, 10,
64, 65; washing and drying, 65, 67

glassware, 62-66, best for tasting, 63;
Champagne, 63; cost, 63; crystal,
67; Crystal d'Arques Oenologue,
63, 65, 66; Grand Jury Européen,
66; Inao, 63, 65, 66; Riedel
Overture, 63-66; Spiegelau, 64

globalization, 137

Grahm, Randall, 161

grains nobles d'Alsace, 164; evolution,
127

grands crus (great growths), 16, 19, 26,
28, 132, 155

grapes: diseases, 151, 157; harvesting,
124, 162, 163, 167-169, 173;
hybrid species, 163; importance of
varieties in wine growing, 14, 136-
138, 142; ripeness, 124, 163, 168,
169, 172-174; skins, pulp and
pigment, 128, 141, 142, 158;
tinting, 141; varieties in Bordeaux
appellations, 154; varieties and
cold climate, 172

great wine, 16, 20; evolution
(Bordeaux, California Cabernets),
126, 127; with food (never with
cheese), 78, 79, 88; mute phase,
129

green pepper aroma, 41, 42, 166

Grenache: aromas, 43; vines damaged
by mechanical harvesting, 169

growing season, 124; in Canada, 162,
163

growths: definition, 16. *See* classified
growths, *crus*, *grands crus*

Guigal (Southern Rhône), 77, red cellar
suggestion, 118; reliable producer,
138

H

half-bottles: cellar suggestions, 115; for
preserving opened wine, 56; in
restaurants, 98

harsh tannins, 21, 35, 36, 57, 72, 87

harvesting, 124, 126, 167-169, 172;
and climate, 124, 135, 136, (in
Canada), 162, 163; icewines and
late harvest, 164; at night, 168

herbal/vegetal, 45, 48, 123, 145, 163,
168; **aroma category**, 41

Hermitage (Northern Rhône): aromas,
39; with food, 78; red cellar
suggestion, 114, 117; white,
evolution, 126

house wine in restaurants, 97, 98

humidity: in conserving, storing wine,
108, 109, 112, 125; in growing
wine, 124, 135, 136, 168

I

ice bucket, 98, 99

icewine, 162, 164; aromas, 42;
Canadian, 161, 163, 164; cellar
suggestion, 121; with cheese, 81;
crystals in, 99; dry before sweet
rule, 61, 65; evolution, 127;
expensive, 121, 164; freshness from
acidity, 164; preservation after
opening, 58

Inao glass. *See* glassware.

improvement of wine in recent times,
124, 172, 173

insects: control of, 157; in juice at
harvest, 168

insuring wine, cellar, 130-132

Internet: Quebec liquor commission
site, 60; consulting for wine
information, 114; for tasting
partners, 14. *See also useful wine
sites in Bibliography*

Italian wines: aromas, by region, 43;
astringency, acidity, 17, 137; with
cheese, 81; dry, cellar suggestions,
114, 115, 117; with meat, 87;
reliable producers, 140; robust
reds, evolution, 127; with spicy and
robust food, 89, 90; sweet, cellar
suggestions, 120, evolution, 127;
white, with fish, 79. *See also*
Piedmont, Tuscany, etc.

J

Japanese condiments with wine, 82, 89
Jumilla (Spain): red cellar suggestion, 120, 138
Jurançon (S.W. France): sweet white, with cheese, 88; cellar suggestion, 118

L

label: back labels, 72, 146, 147; indicates dryness, 80, 82; let guests see it, 72; mildewed from humidity, 108; unregulated information, 150; wine's ID card, 8, 9
Languedoc-Roussillon: aromas, 43; half-bottles for cellar, 115; organic and biodynamic wine, 157, 158; reds, cellar suggestions, 118, evolution, 126; reliable producers, 139
late harvest wines, 169; Canadian, Chilean, 121; German, 119, with cheese, 88; South African, cellar suggestion, 121
leftover wine (conserving it), 56, 57
length, 13, 24, 35 (definition)
Lichine, Alexis, 105
light body, flavour, 33, 34; with food, 86, 87, 90
Lillet Blanc, 85
liquor comissions, control boards. See wine stores; SAQ
Loire Valley: biodynamic wine, 158; dry white, cellar suggestions, 118, with cheese, 61, 81; minerality of, 165; red with Eastern European food, 90, with fish and shellfish, 79, 83, 86; reliable producers, 139; sweet white, cellar suggestions, 118, 120, with cheese, 88; white, evolution, 126, 127
longevity. See evolution

M

Madiran (S. France, tannic red), 36; aromas, 42; with cassoulet, 83; cellar suggestions, 118; evolution, 127
maple syrup aroma, 49
Marches (Italy): cellar suggestions, 118; reliable producers, 140

marijuana aroma, 11, 37, 39, 41
Maury (Roussillon): dessert wine cellar suggestion, 120; evolution, 127; maple syrup aroma, 49
mechanical harvesting, 167-169; cost, 167, 168; pollution, 168
Merlot: aromas, 42; California, Chilean, with oriental food, 89; Chilean, cellar suggestion, 119; evolution, 126; typical character, 138
metal caps, 25, 26, 104
microbullage, 145
microwave oven, 55
mildew: on vines, 157; on labels, 108
Mondavi, 138, 139
Moscato di Passito di Pantelleria (Italy): dessert wine cellar suggestion, 120; evolution, 127
Moulin-à-Vent (Beaujolais): evolution, 126; red cellar suggestion, 117
Mourvèdre: aromas, 43, 48
mouth, 12, 13, 16, 35 (definition); feel in mouth, 12; four basic taste sensations, 12, 28; length, 13; spitting, 29; sucking in air, 13. See also palate
Muscat: Alsatian dry, with asparagus, 83; Australian, cellar suggestion, 121; Beaumes-de-Venise, with hors d'oeuvres, 85; with cheese, 81; conserving after opening, 58; evolution, 127; grape and cold climate, 163; grape juice aroma, taste, 35, 166, 167; not before dry red, 61, 85
mute phase of wines, 10, 21, 35, 72, 116, 122, 129, 130

N

nervosity, liveliness, crisp acidity in white wine, 61, 79, 81, 86, 147
New World wines: aromas, 42; dessert wine cellar suggestions, 121, evolution, 126, 127; oaked not good with cheese, 81, 88; reds with Oriental food, 89; robust with strongly flavoured food, 98; rosés with red meat, 87; whites, as apéritif wines, 61, with cheese, 61, with white meat, 80. See also Australia, Canada, etc.

New World wines compared with Old World wines: competitive advantage (less regulation), 154; fruitier, darker, 17, 80, 98, 137; heavier use of oak, 144, 145; labels more detailed, 146; more emphasis on grape variety, 138

Niagara Peninsula (Ontario): cellar suggestions, 114, 121; Chardonnay, 136; growers and genetically modified vines, 161; icewine, 162, 164; reliable producers, 139

noble rot (*botrytis cinerea*, in Sauternes), 164, 169

North America. *See* New World wines, Canada, etc. *See also* attitudes

nose: definition, 10-12, 35; detects only 3 or 4 aromas simultaneously, 166; easily tired out, 11; superior to technology, 166; taste depends on it, 12. *See also* aromas; odours in wines; sense of smell

Nova Scotia, 163

nymph's thigh (hue of rosé), 36, 37

O

oak: aging, 61, 136, 143-149; American oak: not good with cheese, 81, 88, strong taste from, use in France and Spain, 149; aromas imparted, 88, 39-42, 144-149; cooperage methods, 149; difference, new and old, 148; French oak, 147-149; longevity of reconditioned barrels, 147, 148; oak from other countries, regions, 149

oak chips: planks in vinification, 144, 145

odours in wine, 39; bizarre, unpleasant odours, 11, 26, 37, 39, 42, 64, 95, 165, 166; of cork taint, 24, 41; decomposing vegetation, 11, 42, 48; dishcloth, in glasses, 64; glue and other odours in wine cellar, 107, 109, 111; smell from mouldy barrels, 24; vegetal from debris when harvested, 168. *See also* paint, vinyl, etc.

oenology, oenologists, 172

Okanagan Valley (British Columbia), 162

old vines, 150, 151

old wine: aromas associated with, 11, 16, 48, 123; British preference for, 123, 172; sediment in, 71, 72. *See also* decline

Ontario: cellar choices, 114; Chardonnay, 136; icewines, 162, 164; wine growing in, 162, 163. *See also* Niagara Peninsula

opening: bottle to let wine breathe, 61, 62; bottle (uncorking), 68; Champagne bottle, 68, 69; ritual aspect, 26; one bottle from a batch to verify evolution, 123

organic wine growing, 156-158; taste of organic wine, 158

oxidation, 35 (definition), 104, 105; deliberate (tawny port), 59, 73; effects of, 35, 56, 57, 59; prevented by sulphur, 159

oxygenation, 57, 62, 72, 145

P

paint smell in wine, 37, 64

palate, 12, 13, 24, 35; coated by sweetness, 61, 85; gets tired, 61; length on, 12; refreshed by dry white wine, 81 (footnote); tasting with virgin palate, 46. *See also* mouth

Palmela (Portugal), 138; red cellar suggestion, 120

Parker, Robert, 23

peak. *See* determining readiness; evolution

Pelee Island (Ontario), 163

Peynaud, Émile, 56, 152

Piedmont (Italy): red cellar suggestions, 118; reliable producers, 140; white with fish, 79

pigments, 128, 141, 142

Pineau-des-Charentes: dessert wine cellar suggestions, 120; with hors d'oeuvres, 85; preservation after opening, 58

Pinot Gris: half-bottle cellar suggestion, 115; versatile with food, 87, 98

Pinot Noir: New World, typical aromas, 42, evolution, 126; vines damaged by mechanical harvesting, 169

Pinotage (S. Africa): evolution, 127; robust red cellar suggestion, 120

plum, prune aromas, 42, 43, 123; sign of decline, 128

port: alcohol rate, 59, 105, 108; aromas, 10, 43; with cheese, 81; with chocolate, desserts, 88; colour, 10; in decanter, 771, 73; deliberate oxidation of tawny, 59, 73; evolution, freshness, longevity, 58, 59, 105, 127, 172 (footnote); Quinta do Noval Nacional, 151; reliable producers, 140; serving temperature, 53; with spicy food, 89; storing, 105; sweetness, 85; white with hors d'oeuvres

Portuguese wine: dessert wine cellar suggestions, 121; red cellar suggestions, 120; reliable producers, 140

pouring glass one-third full, 14, 64, 65, 96

Prats, Bruno, 130

precipitation: of anthocyanins, tannins, 128. See also crystals; rain; sediment

preservation after opening: Table, 58, 59; in decanter, 73; in freezer, 57 (footnote); in half-bottle, 57; oxidation, 35, 56-59; upright in refrigerator, 57; with vacuum pump, inert gas, 56-59.

preservation of closed bottles (not in cellar), 103, 104; in dark place, 103, 107; in refrigerator: 99 (footnote), white keeps longer than red in, 103; risks during transportation, 125; temperatures, 103, 107, 108, 125. See also cellar; evolution

producers, 117, 138; reliable producers **Table**, 139, 140. See also wine growers

Provence (France): biodynamic wine, 158; cellar suggestions, 118

provenance (geographical): indicators, 17, 137. See also New World wines compared to Old World wines.

provenance (wine growers): indicates quality, 21, 137, 138, 154, 155

pulp (grape), 141, 158

Q

quality/price ratio, 20, 107, 146; relation to temperature when serving, 54

Quebec: acidic reds, 163; icewines, 164; influence of climate, 162, 163; vine species, 133; white wine, 163; wine growing in, 162-164

R

rain: in growing season, 124; during harvest, 168

readiness of wine: peak, 21, 115, 122-130. See also evolution

red wine: aromas, 41, 42, 44, 48; colour: 10, enhanced in decanter, 72, harmony with red meat, 80, 87, 98, indicates age, 123, 128; decline, 134, 135; evolution, 126, 127; light-bodied with fish, Greek food, 76, 86, 89; not generally good with cheese, 80, 81; preservation after opening, 58, 59; pulp and pigments, 128, 141, 142; serving temperature, 14, 53, 54; sulphur in, 159; and tannins 35, 36, 57, 86, 87; vinification, 141

refermentation in bottle, 155, 159

refrigerator, 55, 99 (footnote), 103

regions (wine). See Bordeaux, Italian wines, Canada, etc.; Tables

restaurants: attitudes of staff, 94-96; half-bottles in, 98; house wines, 97, 98; intimidated by servers, 95-99; sending back wine, 93-96; sommeliers, 93-95; tasting in, 94-96

Rhône Valley wine, 116, 171; and appellations, 154; aromas, 39, 43; climate, 124; quarter-bottles, cellar suggestion, 115; red and white cellar suggestions, 117, 118; red with beef, 83; reliable producers, 139; white, versatile with food, 87, 98

Ribera del Duero (Spain): red cellar suggestion, 120; reliable producers, 140

Riesling, Alsatian: beeswax, spruce gum and other aromas, 42, 49, with shellfish, 86; German Auslese, 97; grape and cold climate, 163;

sparkling wine: with dessert, 82; with hors d'oeuvres, 85; with oriental food, 89; preservation after opening, 58, 59; white sharpens appetite, 61. *See also* Champagne

spicy aromas, 39, 45, 144; aroma category, 24, 41

spicy food and wine, 77, 89, 98, and beer, 89

spitting out wine: principle and technique, 28, 29

spruce gum aroma, 41, 42, 49

Steiner, Rudolf (biodynamics), 158

stoppers for opened bottles, 35, 56, 58, 59

sugar in wine, 82; addition of (chaptalization), 99, 163, 174; coats palate, 61, 85; content and sulphur, 169; fermentation/alcohol, 163, 174

sulphur, sulphites, 157-159

suppleness, softness of wine, 16, 21, 25, 62, 71, 72, 129, 145, 173

sweat aroma, 39, 43, 48

sweetness: balanced by acidity (in icewine), 164; basic taste sensation, 12; doesn't mean fruity, 35; and dryness in white, 147; of New World wines, 17, 137; not after dry, 65; not before dry, 61, 85; of port, 85; sweet aroma category, 41; sweet wine with dessert, 82; taste for in past, 173, 174

swirling technique, 10, 64, 65

Sylvaner (Alsace): aromas, 42, 49; with sauerkraut, 83

Syrah: aromas, 38, 43; 153; assemblages, 138

T

tannins: absent in white, 97, 141; and decline, 128; definition, 35, 36; essential in red, 21, 35, 36; and fish, 86; harsh, 35, 46, 72; and health, 171; and rare meat, game, 87; ripe/unripe, 25, 35, 124, 173; softening, 21, 57, 62, 72, 145; toned down by food, 87, 125

taste(s): acidic, 61; alcoholic, 17, 54; aromatic persistence, 13, 35; basic taste sensations, 12; of corked

wine, 24; deteriorates with oxidation, 59 (tawny port), 123, 128; diluted, thin: 13, 24, 35, 61, 173, by rain, 124, 168; getting used to, 61; of great wine, 20; national preferences, 123, 172; of New World wines, 17, 98, 123, 137, 129, 145, 163, 164; from oak (vanilla, wood, etc.), 144, 149; of old wine, 16, 123; of organic wine, 158; overpowering in foods, liquors, 80-82, 85, 88; rough (from crystals), 99; sweeter in past, 173; of young wine, 21, 128, 129. *See also* flavours

tasting partner(s), 8, 14

temperatures (in serving and preserving wine): allowable fluctuations when storing, 108, 125; cellar temperatures, 107, 108, 110, 111, 123; chilling in refrigerator, freezer, 53-55; and crystals, sediment, 99, 123; ideal for drinking, 53, 54, relation to quality of wine, 54; room temperature, 14, 53, 54, 65, 103; warming wine, 55, 65

terroir, 12, 135, 136; of oak trees, 148; and classified growths, 155. *See also* soil; climate

toast aroma, 39, 41, 148

Tokay: Aszu (Hungarian), dessert wine cellar suggestion, 121; Alsatian, 115

Torrontés (Argentina): white with asparagus, 83; with oriental food, 89

transporting wine, 125

turbidity, 10, 72, 123, 155

Tuscany: aromas, 43; cellar suggestions, 15, 119; reliable producers, 140

typical character, 154, 155

U

Umbria: aromas, 43; reliable producers, 140

uncorking, 26, 68, 69

undergrowth, mushroom aromas, 16, 41, 42, 123

United States, 162, 171; details on labels, 146; lack of regulation, 158; wine stores, 125 (footnote). *See also* oak, American; California

V

vacuum pump, 56, 58, 59
vanilla aroma, 39-41, 43, 81, 88, 144, 148
varietal wine, 138
varieties (grape). *See* grapes, varieties
Vegetal. *See* herbal/vegetal
Veneto reds: aromas, 43; with cheese, 81 (footnote); cellar suggestions, 119; with Eastern European food, 90; reliable producers, 140
Vidal Blanc grape species (Eastern Canada), 163; beeswax aroma, 42
Vin de Constance (S. Africa): dessert wine cellar suggestion, 121; evolution, 127
vin nouveau: when to drink, 126
vin santo (Italy): dessert wine cellar suggestion, 120; evolution, 127
vinegar: bad with wine, 77, 82, 85; cleaning decanters, 73; odour, taste in wine, 95, 172
vines: age, 150, 151; cultivation (climate and soil), 124, 135, 136, 157, 158; damage by harvesting machine, 168; depth of roots, 150, 157; diseases, pests, 151, 157, 158; genetically modifed, 160, 161; harvesting, 124, 155, 164, 167-169; hybrid species, 151, 163; organic, 157, 158; productive life span, 150, 151, 168; pruning, low yield strategy, 124, 150; resistance in winter, 161, 163; spacing rows, 168; species and variety in wine, 136
vineyards. *See* appellations, classified growths; vines
vinification, 166, 168; in barrels, 143, 144; of red wine, 141; of rosé, 142; of white wine, 141; use of sulphur, 159. *See also* wine growers
vintage(s), 16, 21, 95, 115, 117, 124, 127, 129; charts, 124; improvement in recent times, 124; great vintages, 127 (footnote)
vintners. *See* wine growers

vinyl aroma and tastes, 26, 37, 43; from synthetic cork, 105
visual assessment. *See* colour; clarity
viticulture, 124, 135, 136; harvesting, 162-164, 167-169, 173; organic and biodynamic, 158, 159. *See also* wine growers, decisions.
Vouvray (Loire), 165; dry, evolution, 126; with oriental food, 89; sweet, evolution, 127; white cellar suggestion, 118

W

warming wine, 55, 65
wax tab on cork, 104
weather and quality of wine, 124, 163
wet cardboard odour (corked wine), 24, 41
white wine: acidic, with strongly-flavoured food, 89, 90; as apéritif, 61, 85, 147; aromas, 42, 44; colour indicates age, 123, 128; desirable acidity, 36, 57, 61, 81, 119, 147; dessert wine cellar suggestions, 120, 121; dry with fish, 86, 98, with cheese, 61, 81, 86, with meat, 80, 87, 94, with oriental food, 89; evolution, 119; oaked not good with cheese, 81, 88 (note) or fish, 86; preservation after opening, 58, 59; refreshes palate, 81 (footnote); semi-sweet with fish and cheese, 86, with meat, 87, 89; serving temperature, 53, 54; sharpens appetite, 61; stimulates taste buds, 147; sulphur in, 159; versatile with food, 87, 98; 141, 142; vinification, 149
wine: components (*See* components); different in the past, 172-174; diversity of, 135, 136; a faithful ally, 152; with food (*See* food and wine matches); home-made, 148; living organism, 21, 55, 161, 166; promise, potential of, 21; readiness to drink, 21, 122- 127; speculating in, 132; a world of fascinating aspects, 9. *See also* bulk (ordinary) wine, corked wine, fine wine,

fortified wine, great wine, icewine, etc.

wine counsellors, 9, 114, 132, 135

wine courses, 8

wine glasses. *See* glassware

wine growers (vintners, producers): decisions about aging in wood, 144; about fining and filtering, 155, 156; and laws and regulations, 153, 154; importance of name in choosing wine, 29, 137, 138, **Table**, 39, 40, 154, 155; strategies, skill in viticulture, vinification, 136, 138, 142, 150, 155, 157, 158, 173, 174

wine growing. *See* vinfication; viticulture; wine growers

wine guides, 114, 124, 138. *See also* buying wine

wine stores: liquor boards, commissions, 8, 9, 17, 68, 106, 125, 132, 135; reimbursement policies, 125; wine accessory stores, 49, 63, 112

wine tasters: confident, 11, 12; influence each other, 14, 46, 47

wine tasting: ability, 5, 22, 23, 26, 27; assessment steps, 10-13; assessment techniques, 13, 14, 16, 17, 44, 45, 49; attentiveness and concentration, 7, 9, 18, 19, 152; blind tasting, 15-18; confidence, 11, 12, 45; courses and kits, 8, 49; enhanced through practice, 6-9, 14, 40, 44; honesty in, 14, 45-47; ideal conditions for, 18, 19; importance of curiosity, enthusiasm, 6, 7, 10, of intuition, first impression, 11, 46, 47, of memory and patience, 6, 16, of note-taking, 8, 14, 16; judgment affected by glassware, 66; in restaurants, 94-96; snares, 12, 16; threshold of perception, 37; tips for, 11, 14, 21, 44, 45, 137, 138

winery: sorting grapes at, 168; TCA molecules in, 25

woody aromas, 42; **aroma category**, 24, 41; of oaked wine, 144, 148

Y

yeast, 163; designed to enhance fruitiness, 160; fermentation, 141; genetically modified, 160; residual, 155; and variety in wine, 136, 161

young wine: aromas and flavours, 16, 21; French and North American preference for, 123; unidimensional, 128, 129

Z

Zinfandel, 171; evolution, 127; with spicy food, 89; vinyl aroma, 37

This book
set in Hiroshige and Stone Sans 10 on 14
was printed
in October 2003
at AGMV/Marquis,
Cap-Saint-Ignace (Québec), Canada.